QUEER LIFE, QUEER LOVE 3

QUEER LIFE, QUEER LOVE
3

Edited by Matt Bates, Kate Beal, Sarah Beal and Karen McLeod

MUSWELL PRESS

First published by Muswell Press in 2025

Typeset in Bembo by M Rules
Printed and bound by CPI Group (UK) Ltd, Croydon, CR0 4YY

A CIP catalogue record for this book
is available from the British Library

ISBN: 978-1738452859
eISBN: 9781738452866

Muswell Press
London N6 5HQ
www.muswell-press.co.uk

Our authorised representative in the EU for product safety
is Easy Access System Europe, Mustamäe tee 50,
10621 Tallinn, Estonia
gpsr.requests@easproject.com

FSC www.fsc.org MIX Paper | Supporting responsible forestry FSC® C013604

Introduction

Welcome to the third edition of the *Queer Life, Queer Love* anthology. We are delighted to bring together forty new texts that affirm queer lives. Within these pages, you'll find writing which celebrates the richness of the queer experience, exploring characters, themes and encounters that reach beyond the mainstream – embracing the fascinating, the forbidden, the subversive, and even the mundane. In essence, we offer you a view from the outside.

This year we received an overwhelming response to our *Queer Life, Queer Love* 3 call for submissions and we could only feature a fraction of the works. We thank everyone who shared their stories with us. It proves that across the world there are many compelling voices experimenting and sharpening their craft. The work collected in this anthology capture what it means to live as LGBTQI+ people today, exploring the challenges we face and the spaces we call home.

With queer lives continuing to face discrimination and violence around the world, it's more important than ever that our community stands together. This anthology strikes out as a way of encouraging pride, even when there is prejudice. We will always be stronger when united.

Matt Bates, Kate Beal, Sarah Beal, Karen McLeod
October 2025

The Morning After the Night Before – Jon Ransom

I am a thief. Who takes from men at sleep. Souvenirs of sorts. As sometimes I wonder if anything is really real. This is the way of things here. Everything at odds from before. My arms and legs are chicken-skinned because it's cold again, and there could be snow on the ground, but I haven't yet stepped outside. The kitchen table is busy with metallic cans and a scatter of polaroids. Empty cigarette packets, too. I'm writing S . . .T . . .U in fat black letters beneath his picture, before his name goes someplace else and I'm unable to find it. Stu is still asleep in my bed. He doesn't know everything is back-to-front. It might be nice to be Stu, believing his eyes are like windowpanes he looks out of. Him not concerning himself with why he doesn't see two of everything. And upside down.

Pull on my T-shirt I'd hung on the door handle and walk the floor in yesterday's socks, more grey than white. I ease open the bedroom door. The room smells of cum and sleep. Stu is face down, snoring. He's kicked the covers away, tangled about his knees. His grey boxers are the wrong way around, gaping in such a way I can see the crack of his arse my tongue had tasted the night before. Eyes shut, his hairy hole another place, different from the rest of him. Yet with morning, all I care about is his arm, reaching for a sign of something. Maybe me. There's a line of light touching him, travelling all the way to grazed knuckles. I fire off a polaroid. Stu stirs. Put the film beneath my armpit. He rolls onto his back and opens his eyes. Stu doesn't recognise the ceiling or bare bulb, all that I am familiar with.

What the fuck?

I don't want to take another polaroid of Stu. Not now he's awake. It'd be better if he cleared off fast and let me get underwater. I leave him alone in the bedroom, hunting for blue jeans. In the kitchen I load stale bread with butter and salmon paste. Smells like childhood. Wrap the square in bright tinfoil that makes my eyes ache. All the while I can hear Stu striding about. Then his piss hammering the toilet bowl. When he comes into the kitchen his hair is higher than it was the night before, a different colour black. As though the indigo has gone away. Might be I'll find him on the sheet, like an ink stain.

The camera, mate. That shit's fucked up.

Outside, the park is holding its breath. Even the rusty wrought-iron railing has leant in for a closer look. Perhaps the park knows something I don't. Like the time a dead man was found in the fountain, naked. Empty eyes looking at no one. Parks understand things the rest of us can't. I walk into white. From here I can see the brown brick of St. James' pool, past the traffic lights. My swimming trunks and towel are rolled together in a worn carrier bag, sandwich on top. I want to be beneath water. And more.

The boy behind the window has yellow hair. He's new.

Hands me a paper ticket and a red rubber wristband with a brass key attached, locker number 59. Already I can smell chlorine. In the changing room a fat man is sat on the wooden bench in his underwear, tucking socks inside dull shoes. I untie laces. Take off my boots, not worrying because the white-tiled floor isn't yet wet. My clothes I bundle and push inside the bag. Pull on pale-blue trunks and tie the cord. They are the small shiny kind that make me feel like someone else. Someone tan, called Mitch or Cooper. Yet with my winter skin, I look more like the corpse from the fountain. Though I don't mind. In fact, I like it. Hang the rough towel across my shoulder, grazing my nipple. I slide the carrier bag into the locker, careful not to flatten my breakfast. Turn the key and slip the band over my wrist. Then I swim twenty-two lengths. Until my arms feel awkward, like I've borrowed them.

Sat in the observation room, hair half dry, I'm two thirds of the way through my paste sandwich with nothing nice to gaze at. Only old men, stiff in baggy shorts and similar skin. They watch me keenly, watching them. I finish eating and turn in my key. The boy behind the glass wants to know how many lengths I've swam. I shrug. He itches his chin, first flush of stubble. Makes me wonder if his hair is really another colour. Closes his eyes for a long beat. I think his eyelids are nice. A pleasing symmetry of sorts. He asks me what I'm doing later. I smile.

You.

Fat flakes of snow are falling outside. And I reckon this must be what it feels like to be trapped inside a snow globe, like the one Adam gave me two summers before. Adam had everything back-to-front. Winter and summer. Up and down. Here and there. That globe dried up one day. Eventually everything stops being useful. And now I'm climbing stairs to my door, turning the latch behind me. Collect the box from beneath my bed. Sit down at the kitchen table. Clear some space with my arm. Here, I open up the box, rammed with polaroids, too many to count. Too many men. I should put Stu with the others. Instead, I take out a handful, place them before me on the tabletop, one beneath the other. And lastly, the night before.

A . . .D . . .A . . .M
I . . .A . . .N
D . . .E . . .A . . .N
S . . .T . . .U

Jon Ransom's debut, *The Whale Tattoo*, was published to great acclaim and won the 2023 Polari First Book Prize. His second novel, *The Gallopers* won the 2024 Polari Book Prize. His short stories have appeared in many anthologies and journals. He grew up in Norfolk and now lives near Cambridge.

For Sue, whoever she may be – Catriona Knox

I arrive at her door and knock. As usual, she doesn't answer. I try not to take it personally as I genuflect to the letterbox. I push it open.

'Sue, are you in?' It's a dumb question. The only other place she'd be is in hospital. Or dead.

'Hello Sue?'

I really hope she's not dead in there but if she is dead at least I'll get to raise the alarm and feel useful and adrenaline-filled for a few hours. Today marks two years since I began visiting Sue. We were matched on Opening Doors, a befriending charity supporting the older LGBTQ+ community. Her profile read: 'eighty-four-year-old lesbian woman with dementia. Loves animals and musicals.' I circled it with a blue biro. Being the same in all but age felt good enough for me.

'It's Catriona, Sue,' I call out, knowing my name has no meaning for her.

Through the letterbox I see what I always see – a wind-sheeter hanging on the wall, a walking frame and two empty armchairs. The one I'll sit in is covered with a fleecy paw-print blanket. The other, Sue's chair, has a cushion which depicts Audrey Hepburn, replete with *Breakfast at Tiffany's* tiara, pearls and cigarette holder, only Audrey Hepburn is a cat. Out of frame there's a bookcase full of cassettes (all Madonna and Sarah Brightman) and a faded colour printout of a squirrel attached to the wall.

Sue totters into view. She must have been on the loo. No sweat. I call louder, she ignores me, I rap the door, she sits in her chair. Slippers on. Slippers off. Me still banging on the door. This wasn't the way I envisaged bonding with a gay elder. I'd pictured us discussing the hanky code, illicit meetups at the Gateways, Judy Garland's heartbreaking vocal.

'Sue!' I shout, trying not to sound angry even though it's taken me an hour to get here and it will take me an hour to get back and I know this is volunteering but my life matters too and what exactly am I getting out of this right now apart from knee burn?

'Come in dear, it's open.'

'I was knocking,' I say, slightly breathless, shedding my coat and sitting.

She smiles, gives a shrug. It's hard to stay peeved for long.

'How's your mother, dear?' she asks, never having met my mother.

'She's good thanks, Sue.'

'You must send her my love.'

'And she'll send it back,' I say, wondering if it's OK for me to participate in these fabrications. Is the very fact of my being here not a bit, well, abusive? She has no idea who I am or why I come – a friend of Sue's contacted Opening Doors, worried she might be lonely with only carers going in and the occasional visits from friends attempting to manage their own decline. Yet here I am, rocking weekly into her world, forcing her to engage, forcing her into fresh, hellish confusion.

Sue gets up, fetches a glass of water first, then some kitchen roll and finally a packet of Walkers Ready Salted crisps. The items must be fetched one at a time, each collection preceded by her tap routine – a tap of the salt shaker, then the pepper shaker, both again, tap the wooden placemats with birds on and a final double tap of the Dalmatian egg timer. These items exist, the friendly pats seem to say, these are my anchors.

At first, I struggled with the silence, now I love to watch her diminutive, nimble form performing the acts that bring her comfort. I get a kick out of the way she embraces butchness, even at eighty-four – hair a grade two all over, kitted out in a men's shirt and navy slacks. I love the way she nips up the legs of her perfectly pleated trousers before sitting, like a vintage gent. Even though her fly is invariably hanging open, it's a smooth look. She's still got a twinkle. 'I'm allowed people to stay over you know,' she cooed at me the first time I ever visited her.

'So, tell me, how are you, Sue?' I say, leaning forwards, smiling, maintaining eye contact.

'Well of course I haven't been able to sing, you see, because of the phlegm and I was meant to be releasing my album this week,' she says, tutting and rubbing her chin as if feeling for stubble.

'That's not nice is it, phlegm,' I say.

'Because I mentioned it to uh ... whatsername ... oh what's her name, blonde hair, French actress ...'

'Brigitte Bardot?'

'Yes, Brigitte Bardot, that's right. Very beautiful woman. She used to come up here and chat to me. Here she is, on the front here, isn't she stunning?' she says, handing me the packet of crisps, on the front of which is a picture of Mariah Carey.

We laugh and it feels good. Laughing together is communing together, even if you're not laughing at the same thing. It rights the wrongness, makes known the unknown. And it's the known I'm after. Any time Sue hints at her lesbian predilections I'm on tenterhooks hoping she might be about to reveal more . . . a steamy affair . . . a doomed love triangle . . . a former lover turned best friend . . . but it never emerges. Once, at the end of one of our first meetings I noticed a mark on her wrist and, thinking I was keying into comfortable lesbian territory said, 'I like your tattoo.'

'Oh yes,' she replied, 'that's my mother's number. She died in the concentration camps. OK, bye dear, see you next time.'

For days, I couldn't let it go. It seemed urgent to verify it, or engage with it, or at the very least acknowledge it. But I have to be content with never knowing. I must be happy not to be known either. We have no past and no future, Sue and I. We exist only in the slippery, nebulous present.

It's time to sing now. We sing the same songs each week, never tiring of them. First Sue sings 'The Music of the Night' from *The Phantom of the Opera*, followed by 'I Know Him So Well' where she sings both Elaine and Barbara's parts. During the second verse, I put my arms in the air and do a little sway.

But Sue doesn't like it. She shouts and pushes my hands down. It's the first time we've ever touched and I feel more pained by her rejection than I thought I would. This time we share together is unchartered, vulnerable. I can see she's confused, I can see the illness wringing her out of her own mind. I put my hand out to touch her shoulder but she shakes me off, puts her head in her hands.

There are hundreds of thousands of these roller-coaster moments of care happening all over the world right now. That's a queer kind of solace. I steel myself and carry on singing. I ham up the Eliza Doolittle, desperate to ingratiate myself again, '*Oww wouldn't eeeet be larrverly.*'

'Lov-err-ly,' she codas, all forgotten.

'Nureyev, now he was a dancer, and he liked a cock up his arse too,' she shouts, performing a triumphantly smutty arm gesture which could mean arse-fucking and could mean fuck you. I run with the former, laughing to signal that I understand, I'm on her team.

'I'm getting married to my girlfriend next year,' I say, willing her to absorb it, to remember it.

'I'm floating, look,' she says, lifting her arms, then her feet.

I copy her. 'Now we're floating, together!' Maybe it's the fact that we're floating and unknown to one another that allows us to flourish. We're not bound by our successes or failures, there are no fronts – I arrive unwashed, no sartorial choices; she picks her nose, delightedly, in full view, sucking the remnants from her fingers. We're our very own little queer subculture of two. We muddle about in our non-history and there's no grief for the other person because we don't know who it is we've lost. There is joy in that, and freedom. Sue's eyes are closed now.

'What are you thinking, Sue?'

'How does it go? Something about . . . the path . . . going down the path . . .'

Silence and her mouth twitches the way it does when she's recovering a thought.

'Down by the . . .' – a flow of mumbled half-words then, but she is calm, not troubled by it.

'Past the . . . what's the name of that plant . . .? The white one?'

'Snowdrop'? I proffer, 'Cow parsley?'

She opens her eyes wide, fixing them on me and it tumbles out freely, musically now – 'Past the Old Man's Beard, down by the lake and there, in a pool of white light . . .' – she pauses dramatically, eyes brightening with anticipation – 'is Edie standing at the hob.'

'Who's Edie?' I ask, desperate to know, desperate to be the one who can make her remember.

But Sue only giggles, raises both eyebrows and gives a little shrug.

Since writing this, both Sue and Opening Doors have sadly gone. This is in loving memory of them both.

Catriona Knox is an actor, comic and writer, splitting her time between London and Scotland. She recently graduated from the Birkbeck Creative Writing MA and, this is her first published work.

Learning – Dale Booton

you watch videos
of how your kind
do it   bodies
bare & laboured
the slide & smack
of cheek to hip
imagine yourself
inside another
roll hips
thrust groin
into closed hand
practise daily
with new men
each as small
as a minute
& unobtainable
like exploding stars
try to commit them
to memory
so many you want
to watch   so few

you will remember
& none who
will know you exist

Dale Booton (he/him) is a queer poet from Birmingham. His poetry is published by The North and Magma, and anthologised by Broken Sleep Books, Verve, Muswell Press, and Pan Macmillan. He has two pamphlets: *Walking Contagions* (Polari Press) and *On This Stretch of Queerland* (Fourteen Poems). He is a runner-up in the 2024 International Book and Pamphlet Competition.

Reasons to Sleep with a Mop – Luis Lopez Galan

Vera stormed into Paddington Station rather breathless and, as usual, struggled to find the purple lines, so she decided to walk towards the shops instead. The roar of voices muddled her thoughts, making her forget things, and there was nothing she hated more than forgetting. In crowded places and pressing situations, her attention was a beast with a life of its own, fixating on all the wrong things, getting lost. And, to cope, coffee was needed. After exchanging a couple of nods with the young man at the counter, Vera picked up her latte, found a bench to sit somewhere near the loo and pulled out the phone. This was more a necessity than a quirk: before leaving, she would always open the notes on her phone and wander around the flat ticking off a list to ensure every potential danger was neutralised. Plugs switched off, stove turned off, door locked, and so on. Then, whenever the beast that was her attention decided to fixate on unsettling thoughts, she only needed to open the list to calm herself, an exercise that had saved her countless trips back from the tube. It worked most of the time, although her attention would occasionally take control of her body too, making unconscious decisions without warning. It was a four-way relationship: her mind, body and attention on one side, with herself pushed to the corner, merely observing it all unfold.

Had she been too tired when ticking off the checklist? Had she used the oven the previous night? But of course she had, hadn't she? Perhaps she'd now reached a point where the checklist no longer worked, where she ticked away like an automaton. Perhaps the oven was indeed on, and by now its alarm was beeping, warning only an empty flat that wouldn't hold the flames for more than a few minutes. She googled her neighbourhood and scrolled to the News tab. Then her street, her council. But there were no reports of any flat on fire. At least, not yet.

'Come on now, stop it!' she said to herself, or to her mind, or to her body. 'We have no time for this.' And it was true. As she was about to put her phone back into the bag, a message flashed and descended from the top of the screen, a ghostly apparition: *'At what time are you landing, then?'*

Later, on the plane, Vera switched off. Not airplane mode, just off. She sometimes missed the switchboard, where personal phones weren't allowed and news from the outside world had to be monumental to break through: the death of a relative, a terrorist attack. Her supervisor would never have interrupted a shift over a little fire in a flat, Vera thought. And that would have saved her, really, kept her tucked away in a sweet lie where the world wasn't terrible. A lie much like that of the plane, seated and ready to indulge in the worry-blocking comfort of the isolated skies.

And so, she immediately fell asleep, only to wake to the distant but flooding voice of the flight attendant. His was a singing voice, but of a very particular music genre: pop, late 90s or early 2000s. Britney. That was her first thought when the voice swamped her dreams and drew her back into consciousness: Britney.

He was leaving behind uneven waves of laughter as he dragged his trolley down the aisle. Not everyone appreciated his pop-singing voice, but most seemed to. He stopped just two rows ahead of Vera, gesturing theatrically as he handed a cup of tomato juice to the person in the window seat.

'C'mon darlings,' he was saying to the two in the aisle and the middle seats, 'help me out here, will you?' And of course, they did, collaboratively passing the cup as if it were the Holy Grail.

If he had even the briefest moment to charm, he would make use of it. The kind of charm that intimidated ordinary men, thrilled ordinary women, and made extraordinary people feel safe. Now next to her, she waved a timid 'no' with her right hand, but he wasn't having it.

'Not even a water, darling?' he asked, 'Still, sparkling, coffee? A cheeky beer? We're off to Ibiza, after all.'

Coming back to the island was overwhelming enough, so she could only handle it at that time of year, during the off-season, when the clubs were shut, hen dos non-existent, and the villages filled with the long-awaited calm of those who knew the storm would return. It was a matter of months, living in a constant dual state of hating the idea *of* and looking forward *to* the next Summer.

Vera had been born there; technically an islander, though she had spent more time on the island as a visitor than a resident. Her father was a supposed hippy-at-heart from Newcastle who eventually reverted to his more conservative roots; her mother was a posh Londoner who had more deliberately faked a few years of *namaste* and peace-for-the-world in her youth. She came back to England with baby Vera, while he stayed behind and settled in a house lost in the rural north of the island, near San Carlos. No longer a hippy, but a *payés*, a local.

Outside the plane, Vera's body felt the humid air: the forehead instantly damp, the pulse slightly agitated. The mind, however, was somehow at ease and ready to follow Alex's instructions after the text asking at what time she was landing: *follow the road towards the touristy bus stop, turn left, wait by the moto parking, and quickly get into the car.* There one could pull over for a minute without having to pay for a ticket.

The car appeared then, and Vera hurried with her back-pack and all that guilt pressing against her lower back. She always felt guilty when facing Alex, who sat in the car with her poker face, glanced at Vera, and said, 'Hurry up, or you pay.'

She did as commanded and sat up straight, looking at Alex out of the corner of her eye while fastening the seat-belt: her hair was shorter, darker. She looked good, still tanned. Pretty.

'Was it a good trip?'

It had been, but Vera wasn't sure if sharing details was allowed between them. Their long-ended relationship had evolved into an awkward stage of the odd Instagram like here and there, and these drives to and from the airport. Strangely, Alex had become a robust, distant presence in her life, though Vera could barely recall half the memories they had once built together. Of course, the opposite was true for Alex, who would break the silence every now and then, sending a message out of loneliness or horniness, often accompanied by a photo of a place that, Vera assumed, must have meant something to them once. Clueless, she'd leave Alex's messages on read for hours, sometimes days, before replying with a little heart emoji.

'Yes, yes, thanks,' she finally replied. 'It was an OK trip.'

Vera's attention drifted to the sun above as they left the highway. Not summer anymore, but warm enough. Outside the car, an icebreaker: the wind caught the skirt of the second passenger on a bike ahead of them, lifting it to reveal a pink thong in full view. 'Welcome back, now for real,' said Alex, and both broke finally into laughter. Around them, as they made their way north, the island grew greener and quieter, spreading its comforting magnetism; the usual clothes shops lined the roadside, straw baskets, fruit stalls and new constructions waiting for the glory of a next season. Soon they would see the church on top of the hill: white, old, magnificent. Full of memories. When she was over from England for the holidays, Vera used to help her father close the parasols and stack the sunbeds, piling them up and wrapping chains around them for the night. Then, they would climb the hill to witness the pink shades of the August sunset from the church porch.

'Have you thought about it, then?' Alex suddenly asked, one hand on the wheel, the other resting on her thigh. 'You know, the house.'

Vera had indeed thought about it, but she didn't have an answer to the implied question just yet, so it was as if she hadn't thought about it at all.

'We'll see,' she replied, the *we* referring to the fourth way of being she had. 'I need to see myself there on my own, you know?'

'Take your time,' Alex replied. 'I've filled up the car with petrol and left some food in the fridge, though I haven't done much cleaning, you know what I'm like with that . . .'

'Oh, God, no, don't worry!' Vera cut in. 'You didn't have to, please.' And the guilt settled back onto her shoulders.

Four months back, Vera's father had returned to England to die as the proud British citizen he had never been. Alex got the news from her ex-girlfriend's breaking voice over the phone, crying for help from island to island. Someone needed to move the car from time to time, water the plants, and there wasn't anyone else Vera could trust with the spare keys. Now, leaving the sea behind, something possible only mentally on an island, the car meandered along a few sandy roads before stopping by a red iron gate.

'Let me do it,' Vera said as Alex was about to step out. Then, slowly, she got out of the car, walked to the gate, and pushed it: she obviously remembered that it wasn't locked; just an optical trick for strangers. From there, waving back at Alex to carry on without her, Vera started to cover the final few metres on foot. She wanted to breathe in the perfume of pine trees, let the humid air of the early evening brush against her, walk slowly to the house.

It wasn't going to be that bad: the nearest neighbour hadn't changed their Wi-Fi password – Sol234 –, so Vera's phone immediately woke up with what seemed like hundreds of notifications, though they were mostly spam and news, and none of them about a flat on fire in East London. To avoid overthinking, she threw herself into that one activity where she truly managed to keep her attention under control: cleaning. No room for nonsense in it, her focus entirely absorbed by the scents of rocky salt, citrus and bleach. From the sticky kitchen floor to the shelves in the living room, the decorative old boats, the shells. From the dust on the hallway lamps to the bathroom, her favourite place to clean because of the demanding effort required and, therefore, the deeply satisfying reward.

She filled the shower tray with white vinegar and then sprayed it all over the walls. Its powerful smell brought her closer to a blurred understanding of happiness. But her control over her attention was suddenly shattered with a shiver: on the floor, a pair of boot prints faced the sink, as if an invisible body stood there, gazing at its hollow beauty in the impossible reflection. Her father's impossible reflection. The prints were undoubtedly from the boots he'd worn to wander around the fields. She was frightened, but above all felt a mixture of fascination and weariness. She didn't need to deal with that right then; instead, she furiously mopped over them until they vanished. However, a new shiver followed, this time triggered by more concrete evidence: someone was knocking on the door. She put down the mop, removed her gloves, and regretted not having shut the gates. At the door stood the neighbour with the Sol234 Wi-Fi password. Vera remembered her curly hair, but not her name. Yet another Brit who had moved to that other isle decades ago and retained a rich, full-bodied country accent in an English untouched by foreign sounds.

'There you are, love,' said Sol234. 'I knew it was you this time! So sorry for your loss. He was a good man, your dad. I've seen the lights on a few times, mind, but then I'd realise it was the cleaner, wasn't it?'

She meant Alex, but the question remained open, hanging in the damp air.

'I've just arrived, really. Do you . . . want to come in?'

Vera tried to ask, but, before she'd even closed the question, the woman was practically in the kitchen, talking about her dog or her granddaughter; Vera's attention was blocked, overwhelmed. It didn't fully register until the neighbour mentioned that she didn't have much time and would get straight to the point, which was the 'tourist problem'.

'But I thought,' Vera said, 'this was in Barcelona and cities like that, really . . .'

'Well, yes,' the neighbour replied, 'and that's just it, love, we've got to stop it before it gets to that, don't we? We haven't even room for doctors, for heaven's sake, nowhere for folk to live!'

Sol234 had quickly become agitated and, silently, Vera begged her mind, then her body, to stay quiet, just as they used to do with her dad on certain subjects.

'Gotta dash, but here,' said the neighbour, pulling a piece of paper from her jeans pocket. 'Take this and give it a read, yeah? And come to the house anytime, love, don't go quiet on us.'

As the woman grew smaller and smaller down the road, Vera's attention returned to normal and allowed her to read the title on the pamphlet: 'Don't rent to tourists on vacation, rent to locals in need'. And below: 'The next Benidorm? Not on our watch!'. Vera agreed with the sentiment to a certain level yet wanted nothing to do with someone like Sol234. Instead of dwelling on it, she returned to the mop, the bleach, the gloves. But the bathroom no longer smelled of rocky salt. It smelled of her father, or rather, her father's feet. Of that acidic, piercing, and familiar scent of old sweat over fresh sweat from inside his boots. By then, the mop handle was almost becoming part of Vera's hand, but she channelled the energy into frantically scrubbing the prints again, up and down, over and over, for a whole minute. Then, with a creeping fear spreading through her body, the kind one feels when running back to bed after using the loo in the dead of night, she stopped, slammed the door shut, and went straight to bed, where she surprisingly fell asleep still clutching the mop all night.

In the morning, Vera woke up to the sunlight on her eyelids; the shutters were still open. She got up and left the mop tangled in the sheets because, really, what did it matter? Disorientated, as if her mind couldn't quite connect with her body and her attention was still asleep, she remembered the smell in the bathroom, and the footprints. So, to avoid opening that door, she stepped outside the house, walked along the porch, then into the orchard, and reached the bushes that filled the space between two fig trees on the back of the house. There, she pulled down her trousers, relieved herself, and, as she did, decided she couldn't spend the day in the house. *'I will go to the rocks,'* she texted Alex.

By car, it was about ten minutes away. Their existence marked the end of a small *cala* where the sand was reduced to a few secret metres. A cove with gentle waves and a dark blue giving way to turquoise around small, sharply pointed islets. In the past, sitting there, she had forgotten that she even had a mind, and often a body. She had reconciled herself with the idea that she was not the sum of a few parts, but a whole that somehow connected her to the rocks, the sky and the sea.

From the sand, empty at that time, she climbed up to the rocks, stretched out the sarong, and placed the basket beside her before taking out her phone and starting a conversation with Alex.

Vera: at the rocks. Going mad. Last night I freaked out with the ghost of my dad in the bathroom.

Alex: right. You OK, though?

Vera: Yeah. I could smell him. Like he was right there. V odd. I honestly think he's haunting me, you know what I mean . . .

Alex: you're living through a trauma, that's all. He did smell sometimes though. Lol, sorry. Is this the coming-out thing again?

Vera: I never told him.

Alex: He knew . . .

Vera: Not from me.

Alex: so you're coming out to a ghost then? Yelling I'M A LESBIAN in the bathroom?

Vera: so funny!

It's easier than we think to fall into madness, that's what Vera thought, and the thought turned into an awareness. She shouldn't have to deal with everything and a ghost at the same time, or at least not at that moment. She climbed down to the sand as the turquoise around the edges of the rocks faded to pale, almost white, with the reflection of the sun. As she stopped to breathe, she cast a shadow. Not too far, on the other side, where the sand turned into another wall of rocks, protecting the cove from strangers. The shadow shifted into Vera's sight and revealed itself to be that of a naked woman walking somehow gracefully to the calm waves. Surely a local, for she was certainly used to walking on sand. The woman made a couple of yoga-like stretches before stepping into the water. As she did so, Vera's clothes were already scattered around her in disarray. She would rent the house and ask Alex to take care of it, to deal with the tourists, the neighbours and the ghosts. Her mind had made the decision, her body had reassured her, and her attention was fixed on the other naked woman, whom she followed into the sea.

Luis López Galán (he/him) is a writer based in England. He is currently pursuing a degree in Philosophy and regularly reads manuscripts for various editorial projects. Originally from Spain, he writes in Spanish and translates his work into English. His contributions can be found in the blog of the American Philosophical Association (APA) and Epistemic Literary Magazine. On Twitter and Instagram at @llopezgalan

No such thing as forever – Isabel Costello

I was heading down Boulevard Voltaire
in a taxi around 2 a.m.
when the light turned red and there it was
that bar where we used to go
shutters down, designer graffiti
the kind people pay for these days

Those few seconds took me back
however long it's been, I lose count
to your raucous laugh and play on words
the sexy, filthy way you held a glass
the way you wrapped your leg round a bar stool
or around mine in a split skirt

That shade of lipstick I didn't like
but somehow I liked it on you
you'd touch my face and kiss me
in front of everyone
not 'as if it were the most natural thing in the world'
but because it always has been

It didn't last forever, you and me
because there's no such thing

but those nights we braided our hair together
and tied ourselves in knots
That time you invited the concierge's son
and how furious I was till I saw him
We all came so hard the neighbours complained
but they smiled and went red the next morning

Just one day after that taxi ride
I heard news that wasn't new
that unlike me you never grew old
so that's why you stopped calling
I'd always imagined you back in your country
casting your light around

Although you left, you never will be gone
look how you've stepped from the darkness
of a street corner in our old town
to my head, to my pen, to the page
When there's no such thing as forever
all the more reason for now

Isabel Costello is the author of two novels, the acclaimed *Paris Mon Amour* and *Scent*, which was longlisted for the Polari Book Prize. Her short fiction and poetry have appeared in many anthologies including previous volumes of *Queer Life, Queer Love*. Isabel also works as a creative writing tutor, mentor and freelance editor. She has life-long connections with France where much of her work is set and divides her time between London, Paris and Marseille.

Starting School – Sophia Blackwell

The deer crashes out of the trees, not-there and then there, like a lick of fire. Jo, swearing under her breath, brakes as gently as she can. It jars Stella, who's in the back. (Even with Jo's usual perfection, the back seat of her car is the usual chaos of discarded toys, unpaired socks and damp-looking biscuit crumbs that every parent has, and Stella has folded her coat under her to avoid contact).

It's close, but they stop short of the deer. As the three women gather themselves and watch it go, they see that it's limping, its grace distorted into the gait of a smaller animal, a three-legged cat or dog.

'Shame,' Ally murmurs. 'Should we call someone, do you think?'

She's always deferential to Jo, the youngest in their firm's history to make partner. Ally is not a partner, and Stella senses that this doesn't matter to Jo as much as it does to Ally.

'One of the vets, maybe. I'll look it up.' Jo starts the car. 'That's one thing about living in the country. That, and you have to have a car. Amira is climbing the walls, wondering when you two are getting here. It's a long afternoon when you're five.'

Stella clocks the veiled complaint. They'd been late leaving, missed one of the trains to this place (it can't still be London, surely)? and stopped for the loo in a Liverpool Street pub. Stella suggested Ally update their hosts, but either Ally misunderstood her (likely) or couldn't admit to a mistake (more likely) and Jo must have been waiting a while at the station. Still, these are Ally's friends, and Stella may not see them again, so she's not going to worry too much.

'You're liking living here, then?' Stella asks. These trees seem endless. She feels further away than she is from her shared flat in the middle of the public transport hub that is Finsbury Park, or 'Stroud Green' as the estate agents call it.

'Oh, yeah. The only thing is not having friends nearby.' Finally, they pull into the drive. 'I think Cat could do with meeting some new people. Of course, Amira is starting school in a week, so we won't be able to avoid them even if we wanted to. Which I do. But Cat never did any of that NCT stuff when she had Chris and we just sort of fell off the radar when they were babies . . . so thank you for schlepping out here.' Jo helps Stella with the complicated lock on the car door. 'Come in. I'll give you the tour.'

*

The house is substantial and solid, decked out in an influencer's palette of greige, cream and taupe. Everything is aggressively new, but Jo and Cat are just tasteful enough to avoid the white-and-silver look that dominates the high street in Loughton, where Stella's parents live and where she endured a miserable adolescence as the lone Drama Goth among long-lashed Pomeranians.

The kitchen, as Stella expected, is immense, with a white, gold-veined marble-effect island that reminds her of an altar, bearing four champagne flutes and an ice bucket. The woman who turns around from the oven is a stunner, her earthy, olive-skinned beauty apparent even with smudged lipstick, messily piled-up black hair and a flannel shirt and jeans that give her the look of a stay-at-home Mom in a Hallmark holiday movie. She's a few pounds overweight, with rounded hips and a cleavage framed by the cake-slice V of her shirt that makes Stella wonder why she bothers watching her own weight – surely this abundance is nicer to look at than her own slightly lumpy, muscle-deficient skinniness. Perhaps if she was married, Stella could let herself go. She pictures herself sitting on an oversized sofa in a bigger, more comfortable body, eating deep-fried nibbles, but she's still clinging onto her 'market weight'. This irritates Ally, who keeps buying her cheese as though a few extra pounds will keep her in their bed. Jo is also big, but in a way that seems as though it would be impossible for her to ever be smaller, her whole body seemingly carved from high-shine teak. Ally is stocky, neatly packaged in her black shirt and chinos, but she is older than Stella and probably only has a few years before things start to slide.

There's something familiar about Cat, and as the woman reaches over the kitchen island to give her an awkward air-kiss, Stella realises where she's seen her before.

An Edinburgh gay bar, CC Blooms, on the final night of the Festival, a Last Days of Rome feeling of hedonism in the air. Some were enjoying their success – Stella was, with a play of hers that hadn't gone too badly – or drowning their sorrows from a show that had started falling apart two weeks before.

Stella remembers Cat's slimmer body on stage, twisting sinuously to the brassy beat and flow of the 'St James' Infirmary Blues'. She'd gone out to smoke in an alley, the brunette who'd been on stage stopping next to her. *Excuse me, do you have a light?*

A house, rented for August, in the New Town. White sheets. White ceilings.

'Nice to meet you,' Cat says in her ear. 'I'm Catalina.'

Her voice sounds firm, but Stella isn't sure if it's an instruction – and, after a year of dating Ally, she's used to those.

*

Amira is a gorgeous child with pale-brown skin and a tangle of tea-coloured curls. Despite her excitement about seeing them, she's tongue-tied as Cat and Jo try to get her to talk about starting school.

'Chris is with his dad for the weekend,' says Cat, without the rancour that Stella usually hears when her friends say things like that. She imagines they have a civilised arrangement, if the photo of six people on the kitchen counter is anything to go by – Cat, Jo, the kids and two aftershave-ad-looking men who are either gay or just very comfortable with matching festive pyjamas, as is everyone in the picture, apart from Jo who looks like she'd rather be in a suit.

Cat pours champagne. 'I wasn't going to drink tonight, but . . .' Stella isn't sure what she's going to say, 'what the hell.'

At first, Stella doesn't get to speak to Cat much, as she's ferrying dishes back and forth from the oven – she seems to have made enough for an Italian wedding. Over dinner, the conversation is jerky, with Ally and Jo discussing true crime podcasts while Cat tries to encourage her daughter to eat, though Amira's main interest is dessert and when it might be served, a subject she keeps returning to despite having no appetite for potatoes, pasta or the cold chicken nuggets her other mother is looking at hopefully. At one point, Amira brings a music box to the table and, sitting next to Stella, starts banging out the tunes like an enthusiastic DJ.

'I don't think Stella wants to hear that right now,' says Cat reasonably, and though it's true, Amira bursts into broken-hearted sobs and Stella feels horrible.

'Witching hour,' says Cat with an eye-roll, and stands up to get her daughter some pavlova. They tactfully don't allude to the fact that it's probably past her bedtime because of their guests' child-free timekeeping.

As Stella washes up, she sings a snatch of an old Gomez song that's been stuck in her head all day. 'Sorry, I'll stop,' she says, when she sees Cat looking at her as she dries a glass.

'No, it's pretty. You know what we should do? Jo?' She looks towards the table. 'When Amira is . . .' she indicates up the stairs, 'can you fire up the karaoke?'

*

Once they're on their feet and singing, the gathering takes on a looser, more chaotic style and Jo and Cat revert to being youngish women, Cat telling stories about her burlesque days and demonstrating a routine (clothes on) to Peggy Lee, the words scrolling behind her on their huge flat-screen TV. Stella watches her face for clues that she remembers New Town.

Jo, who smokes rather than drinks, rolls a joint and Ally tucks in; Stella doesn't, but she knows she's making quite a dent in their wine fridge. Jo raps a credible 'My Shot' from *Hamilton,* 'I can't dance at the same time, though, not when I'm high.' Ally gives a surprisingly sweet rendition of a Joni Mitchell song and Stella brings out one of her old audition pieces, 'All That Jazz' from *Chicago.* Then Cat, after some slightly drunken scrolling through the songs, sings Carole King's 'Will You Love Me Tomorrow'. When she can, and when the others are looking away, she lets her eyes rest on Stella's face and finally allows herself a full smile.

'Nice,' Jo says, and her innocence makes Stella feel bad for a moment.

'Very Amy Winehouse,' Ally agrees.

'Who's up next?' Cat turns away. Stella takes another gulp of wine.

*

It's long past midnight, and Jo and Ally are in their respective beds. Amira, who came downstairs after a bad dream, is poured across Cat on the sofa, the two of them like a Pietá, the child having crashed out again as soon as she hit her mother's lap.

'You don't have to worry,' says Stella. 'I don't think I'll be around for long.'

'That's a shame.' Cat doesn't pick up on why she might be worried, and Stella likes that she doesn't make them go through more play-acting.

'I should never have said I'd be exclusive with her. We weren't even . . . you know, it wasn't a big polygamy thing with spreadsheets, I wasn't even sleeping with anyone else before we made it official. I just thought that would make her happy, that she'd stop fighting with me, or at least that the breaks between arguments would be longer.' Stella knocks back the honey-warm dregs of her wine. 'But now I can't get a text, can't chat with one of my exes without it all kicking off. People I used to work with, even. I swear, people go into marriages with lower levels of commitment – and marriages go wrong, too.'

'Tell me about it.'

'But you and Jo are happy, aren't you?'

'We are. But she's just so all-consumingly focused, and some of my stuff tends to fall by the wayside. Sometimes I want to say to her, "You're a lawyer advising dodgy companies, not an A& E doctor." She never said she was, in fairness. And neither am I.'

'Are you working at all, or . . .?'

'Bit of interior design, like most of the wives round here. I make about ten thousand a year. A regular Mr Darcy.' Stella can tell she's said it before.

'How long have you been together?'

'Ten years. You can tell Jo, if you like. We were on a break, to quote *Friends.* The IVF wasn't working, and we couldn't stand the sight of each other. Jo wanted to start adoption proceedings. Which we did, after Chris,' she indicates Amira, 'but at that time, I wanted, literally, another shot. In the middle of all this my friend Holly called from Edinburgh and told me her mum was ill, and she'd get blacklisted if she didn't get cover for a couple of days, so . . . to be honest, I don't think they would have missed another girl with a big bum taking her clothes off.'

'I would have. Was I your last holiday?'

Cat smiles. 'My hen party, maybe. We somehow managed to get married after that, and . . . I think we would have muddled through, regardless of what happened with the kids. But we were lucky.' She looks down at Amira. 'Sometimes, when she's like this, I can see her baby face. Not that I knew her then, but I like to think I'd know it if I saw it.'

'She's got it all in front of her,' Stella says. 'Like I've got it all behind me.'

'Come on, you're what, thirty?'

'Thirty-two. It's a bit of a nothing age, really.'

She doesn't say what she's thinking, which is that while she never wanted the comfortable, respectable lifestyle that these two have, there doesn't seem to be another option, no circus to run away to. It's as if she's living in the nineteenth century – in order to move forward, she has to link up with someone, form an alliance, pool resources. And it can't be Ally. They're just arguing too much, and she has the sense that, if she ever had a chance to address what was wrong with them, it was some months back and she was probably too scared to do it. Sometimes, though not often, Ally looks at Stella as though she actually hates her.

She feels irrationally jealous of the child in front of her, even though her own schooldays were a heady mix of boredom, powerlessness and frustration, glass-sheened toilet paper, ploughing with her desk-mates through the same three pages of *The Ghost of Thomas Kempe* and being shoved in the corridors by prettier girls. As a child, Stella had never liked being told what to do, but at this point, she would pay someone to give her a way out of the corner she's backed herself into.

'I like being your hen party. I bet it's like another life to you now.'

'No,' Cat says, raising her eyes from her daughter's face. 'It's the same life.'

When Stella goes upstairs and stumbles into the guest room, she sees Ally's back to her and fears the worst, but once she gets into bed, Ally turns around to her and pulls her close.

*

'I am actually dying,' says Cat, in the back seat with Stella and Amira as the child stabs happily at a squeaky game on the iPad that keeps trying to sell her things that Jo and Cat tell her she can't have. 'I can't believe we've got that "starting school" picnic later. I am hanging out of my . . . anyway.'

'Oh yeah, I'd forgotten about that.' Jo is driving again, not apparently as badly affected as the rest of them. 'Are we meant to be bringing food?'

'Well, I was going to cook, but . . . no. We'll have to pick something up.'

It's an insultingly beautiful morning, though none of them are in any fit state to appreciate it.

'Oh, I forgot about that deer,' Jo muses. 'The hurt one. I wonder what happened to it.'

'What deer, Mumma?' asks Amira.

'Never mind, baby, I'm sure it's fine.'

But Amira asks again and again, and just when they think she's forgotten she asks one more time, or murmurs to herself about it, wondering. Stella remembers that feeling as a child – the anxiety, the huge compassion, the feeling that her mind had nothing to fasten onto apart from one thing that had gone wrong, one thing she was powerless to heal.

Stella forces herself to open her eyes and distract Amira by asking her about the game, if she's excited about seeing her friends later. Cat pulls her sunglasses down from the crown of her head and over her eyes.

The road pours itself out in front of them, with no end in sight. Stella knows it will end, of course, it has to. She just doesn't know when.

Sophia Blackwell's poetry has been published by Bloodaxe, Nine Arches and the Emma Press among others, and her writing has appeared in Mslexia. She is the author of *The Poetry Writer's Handbook* from Bloomsbury and teaches as part of the Writers' and Artists' team.

The Long Haul – Matt Cain

April 2015

Stuart drives his truck off the train and away from the Channel Tunnel. After passing through tall fencing topped with razor wire, he gives his usual nod to the sign that says, 'Welcome to France'. Within minutes, he's on the motorway – or *autoroute* as the signs call it. Northern France isn't the prettiest part of Europe but Stuart's happy to be on the open road, where he feels free but also sheltered from the world in the safety of his cab, his only company the meditative hum of the engine and the sound of the truck's wheels rolling over the tarmac.

Sitting on the dashboard, the job sheet catches his eye. Written on the outside of the brown envelope are the headlines. *Driver: Stuart Tonge. Destination: Munich.* Stuart doesn't want to look at the date. He tosses the envelope over his shoulder, onto the bed behind him.

Tomorrow, it'll be thirty years since the incident that changed his life, the incident that led to him retraining to become an HGV driver, but also to him withdrawing from the world.

At the age of fifty-six, Stuart doesn't accept many long-haul jobs anymore. The back and leg ache have become too much for him and he struggles with tiredness. *But right now I just want to get as far away from home as possible.*

February 1984

It's a Friday night and Stuart is in High Society, waiting to meet his friends. He looks out over a dance floor that's lit up by multi-coloured tiles and packed with men moving and jerking their bodies to Heaven 17's 'Temptation'. The air is heavy with cigarette smoke, laced with Kouros after-shave, and crackles with sexual anticipation. But Stuart isn't feeling it.

He should be brimming with confidence as he's wearing his best checked lumberjack shirt – what he calls his 'pulling shirt' – his trusty pair of Levi 501s, heavy-duty Doc Marten boots and a new leather jacket. But he's had a tough day. He's employed by Manchester City Council, where his job is to erect signs, barriers and temporary traffic lights before road works or after accidents. His colleagues are all male, most of them are macho, and their chat is often homophobic. Today he was subjected to a particularly bad outburst. As usual, it had to do with AIDS: gay men were accused of spreading the disease, putting innocent people in danger, deserving everything they had coming to them. As nobody at work knows Stuart is gay, he kept quiet. But he's not sure how much longer he can do that. He'd like to leave his job but he doesn't know what else he could do. Unless he found a job in a gay bar or a club like High Society he's pretty sure he'd come across homophobia. *It's everywhere – and it's getting worse.*

On the other side of the dance floor, a man catches his eye. He's leaning on the Pac-Man table, telling his friends a joke that that ends with a punchline that makes them erupt in laughter. The man's gorgeous and looks a bit like Simon Le Bon. *But there's no point – he's way out of my league.*

As the record playing changes to Miquel Brown's 'So Many Men, So Little Time', a cheer rises up from the dance floor. Stuart goes to the bar.

When he returns, he's surprised to find the Simon Le Bon lookalike standing waiting for him. 'You could have got one for me,' the man chirps.

Stuart looks down at his pint. 'Oh. Sorry.'

'Only jokin',' the man says, 'I've got one.' He holds up a glass of what he tells Stuart is a *piña colada*. 'It may be pissing it down outside but at least I can pretend I'm on the beach in a Bounty advert.'

Stuart spots the opportunity to flirt. 'Bounty's coconut, i'n't it? That's pineapple.'

The man grins at him. 'Oh what do I know? I grew up on a farm in Staffordshire. The most exotic place I've ever been to is Rhyl.'

They laugh. Stuart feels his bad mood lifting.

'I've seen you in 'ere a few times,' the man goes on, twirling the umbrella in his drink. 'Let's just say you caught my eye.'

'Oh yeah? Stick out, do I?' says Stuart.

The man looks at his crotch. 'No, you're alright. For now, anyway.'

Their eyes meet and a tingle runs up Stuart's spine. *I can't believe he's flirting with me.*

'I love your 'tache,' the man goes on. 'And you're a solid block of a bloke, just how I like 'em. What's your name?'

'Stuart. But most people call me Stu.' He holds out his hand.

The man doesn't take it but kisses Stuart on the cheek. 'Pleased to meet you. But sorry, I need to get back to my mates. One of 'em's just been dumped by some dickhead he was seeing and we're doing our best to get 'im over it.'

'It's alright, I get it,' replies Stuart. 'What's *your* name?

The man smiles. 'Jack. As in, "Come back".'

Stuart returns his smile. 'You seem very sure of yourself.'

'Have I reason not to be?' Jack holds Stuart's gaze and his eye gives a twinkle.

'We'll see.' But even as he says the words, Stuart's hoping Jack *will* come back.

April 2015

Stuart drives down the *autoroute* at a relaxing 53 miles per hour. He passes the spot where he had a blow-out in his first year of driving and had to pull over on the hard shoulder. It was a frightening experience and knocked his confidence for a while.

He considers how much he's changed since those early days – and how much the job has changed too. For a start, there were no mobile phones or satnav. And he used to drive a truck with a fixed chassis – or a 'rigid' as they're known – before passing his test to drive Class 1 vehicles. He can remember being surprised to find it's actually easier to drive one of the bendy trucks than it is a rigid, that they're much easier to manoeuvre. This gives him a pleasant feeling of being in control.

Stuart taps out a beat on the steering wheel. Soon he'll be crossing the border into southern Germany. He looks at the time on the tachograph control pad that records how many hours he's been driving, as well as his breaks and rest periods. Although it isn't dark yet, he's going to have to stop in an hour or so: it's coming up to the maximum nine hours he's allowed to drive in one day.

He thinks of where he should park for the night. Not far away is a big truck stop that has a cruising ground in the bushes beside it. During his early years as a driver, Stuart used to love stopping there and would look forward to it all through France. He liked his sexual encounters anonymous and fleeting, with men from all over the world he knew wouldn't ask for his number. But lately, cruising grounds aren't as busy as they used to be: if any of the drivers want what they've started to call a 'hook-up', they tend to do it via Grindr or one of the other phone apps. Plus, Stuart doesn't get as much attention as he used to. He shaved off his moustache when it fell out of fashion, his thickset frame has softened, and his brown hair has disappeared, leaving him completely bald. He has developed a certain appeal as a 'daddy', but he isn't interested in much younger men.

These days, Stuart's more interested in the chicken schnitzel and chips they serve in the truck stop café. *Yeah, that's what I'm going to do – have a chicken schnitzel. Then I'll get back to my cab, plug in the kettle and have a nice brew.*

October 1984

Stuart sits next to Jack on a boulder beside the path. He takes out a flask of tea, pours it into a cup and hands it over. For a moment, the two men fall silent, enjoying the view of the open moorland and wooded valleys of the Peak District.

'Now, aren't you glad you came?' Jack says, teasingly.

'Yeah, alright,' Stuart replies. 'You win.'

Jack elbows him in the ribs. 'Next time, don't put up such a fuss!'

Stuart rolls his eyes in exasperation. But the truth is, he only pretended he didn't want to come for a walk because he enjoys bickering with Jack: it makes him feel like he's part of a normal couple. That's all he ever wanted when he was growing up, to be part of a couple like his mum and dad, only with another man rather than a woman. But all the adults he knew said queers couldn't love, that all they did was have dirty, depraved sex that everyone was quick to point out they found disgusting. When Stuart told his family he was gay, they disowned him. At least he'd left Blackburn by then and had already moved to Manchester. Jack had it much worse because he was still living at home. His parents kicked him out, without a scrap of compassion. When he made it to Manchester he had to sleep on a bench in Piccadilly Gardens then spend a few weeks in a homeless hostel before finding a job as a gardener in Heaton Park. Although Jack loves the city's gay scene and its sense of community, Stuart knows he's a country boy at heart. *That's why he craves days out like this.*

Jack passes the tea back to Stuart and he drinks it then tops it up. As they go back to admiring the view, hundreds of swallows swoop up into the sky, swirling and gliding around each other as if performing a dance.

'They must be ready to go back to Africa,' says Jack. 'Leaving home for another year.'

'Yeah but *is* this their home?' asks Stuart. 'Or is it there?'

'Well, they were born 'ere.'

Stuart lets out a breath. 'That don't mean owt.'

Jack frowns. 'I've never thought of it like that.'

Stuart turns to face him. 'Speaking of home, I wanted to talk to you about summat.'

'Oh yeah?'

He has a sip of tea and passes the cup to Jack. 'Well, our living situation i'n't ideal, is it?'

Jack screws up his nose. While he can only afford to live in a bedsit with a single mattress on the floor, Stuart's landlord has said he won't tolerate two men staying in the flat – so if they want to spend the night together they have to sneak Jack out in the morning. As Stuart knows several other gay men who've been in this position, he's aware that the law offers them no protection – and is worried he'll be served an eviction notice.

'My lease is up in t' spring,' he goes on. 'Why don't we find somewhere new – somewhere we can live together?'

Jack inches towards him. 'Really?'

Stuart can't read his expression and is worried that he isn't keen. Over the last few months, he's realised that the flirtatious Jack who approached him in High Society was actually all a front. Behind that he's quite shy, likes tending the flowers in the window boxes he's put in his bedsit, and filling his sketchpad with drawings of animals and birds. *What if he doesn't want to move in with me?*

'Yeah,' he says, trying not to sound desperate. 'I'm not saying it'll be easy but we can ask around and see if anyone knows any landlords who accept two fellas. We know a few guys who do it so there must be some.'

Stuart looks at Jack and is pleased to see he's smiling.

Jack takes a swig of tea and hands the cup back to Stuart. 'Alright, you're on.'

Feeling buoyed up by happiness, Stuart looks around to

check there are no other walkers. He moves in to kiss Jack on the lips.

April 2015

As Stuart walks back to his truck from the café, he feels the satisfaction that comes from having a good meal. *That chicken schnitzel were every bit as good as I remembered.*

He passes the entrance to the cruising ground and notices a few men stepping through and disappearing inside. Through the bushes, he can see the torch from a phone being waved around and someone igniting a cigarette lighter. It looks busier than it has for a while and Stuart feels a fluttering in his stomach.

But no, I couldn't. Not today.

Under a streetlight by the entrance, a man is sitting on the railings and tugging on one of those new vapes. Stuart slows his pace to get a look at him and sees he's probably in his forties and mixed-race. *Or maybe North African?* Not that it matters: he's out of Stuart's league.

The man catches his eye and holds his gaze.

Hold up, is he giving me the come-on?

The man beckons with his head, stands up and slopes off into the cruising ground.

Stuart finds himself following. It's like he can't help but be drawn in. His heart rate soars and the adrenaline surges through him.

He pursues the man down a narrow path, lined with a few dozen other men standing around looking for action. A handful of them have already found it and taken their partners – or small groups – into the overgrowth.

No-one's making much noise, other than a faint groaning that can just be heard over the sound of the traffic from the *autobahn* – along with the tinkle of belt buckles being undone. Although it's been years since Stuart was here, he recognises the urgent, brutal desire that's electrifying the atmosphere.

The man he's following steps into a clearing and Stuart goes after him, a twig snapping under his foot.

Although it's dark, he can just about make out the man's face. He's even more gorgeous than he thought.

The man nods at him. Stuart undoes his jeans.

The man undoes his and moves in to kiss Stuart.

But Stuart shakes his head. He turns the man around.

April 1985

Stuart rushes down Princess Street to meet Jack. A few hours ago, his new landlord called him at the office to say he could pick up the keys to the flat he and Jack are renting from him. He couldn't resist nipping across town to grab them before rushing home for beans on toast, a quick bath and a change of clothes. But he doesn't want to be late as Jack's always early. *And I can't wait to see the look on his face when I show him the keys.*

They're meeting on the corner of Canal Street and Sackville Street, opposite The Rembrandt, the pub where they always begin their Friday nights. But Jack prefers to meet outside as he doesn't like going into the pub on his own. Stuart doesn't mind: he loves walking through the doors with Jack on his arm.

As he turns and walks up Canal Street, he looks at his

watch and is relieved to see he's on time. But as he approaches the bridge, he becomes aware of some kind of kerfuffle. *What's going on?*

Before he can find out, a group of skinheads races past him. 'Fucking queer!' one of them shouts to his friends, who scoff and snigger.

Stuart's insides give a lurch. *They're not talking about Jack, are they?*

He jogs over to the bridge, where a group of people have gathered. A woman is wailing hysterically while another quietly sobs, comforted by her boyfriend. Stuart pushes his way through and sees Jack, lying on the pavement. A bolt of terror shoots through him.

He drops to his knees, into the blood pooling around Jack, and cradles him in his arms. 'Jack, are you all right?'

There's no reply.

'It's me, Stuart,' he says.

Jack's head flops back in his arms. His eyes are open and Stuart detects the faintest blink.

'Can somebody call an ambulance?' he shouts.

A man he vaguely recognises steps forward. 'They've already done it in t' pub.'

Someone else he knows from the Rembrandt shouts, 'Come on, give 'em some space!'

As the woman who's wailing is guided away, everything goes eerily quiet. Stuart loses all sense of where he is or of time passing. It's as if he isn't really present, as if he's having some kind of hallucination.

He needs to re-engage.

He takes hold of Jack's hand. 'I've picked up the keys to t' flat,' he whispers in his ear. 'I were going to surprise you.'

Stuart is sure Jack gives his hand a tiny squeeze.

He carries on. 'The landlord says it's fine to bring your window boxes.'

Am I imagining it or was that a little smile?

'We're going home, Jack,' Stuart continues. 'You and me. Just like them swallows.'

He kisses him on the forehead but Jack gives no response.

The blare of a siren indicates the ambulance is arriving.

'Clear the area, please!' shouts a tall man in uniform.

Stuart loosens his grip on Jack as two men step forward, kneel down and begin pressing and prodding him.

'We've got a young white male, multiple stab wounds,' the shorter of them says into a walkie talkie.

The tall one turns to Stuart. 'And who are you, pal?'

Stuart hesitates for a moment. *Should I say 'a friend'? Or is it safe to tell the truth?*

'I'm his boyfriend,' he says.

Stuart spots fear darting through the eyes of both men.

'So he's queer, is he?' the tall one asks.

'What's that got to do with owt?' Stuart protests.

'A lot,' responds the shorter paramedic. 'In case you haven't noticed, there's a lot of blood 'ere. I'm sure you've heard of AIDS?'

Before Stuart can reply, the taller paramedic returns to the ambulance and brings out more protective gear. The two of them are already wearing gloves and aprons but put on masks and overalls that cover them from head to toe. They lift Jack onto a stretcher.

'Can I come with him?' asks Stuart.

'Sorry, it's family only.'

'But his family don't speak to him,' Stuart pleads. 'And I can't leave him on his own.'

'You're going to have to, pal,' says the taller paramedic, in a tone that indicates the matter's closed.

They ask for Jack's name and Stuart gives his details. 'At least tell me where you're taking him.'

As the man gives him the name of the hospital, Stuart feels a hand on his arm. 'Come on, let's get you a taxi.'

Stuart desperately wants to kiss Jack – this time on the lips – but he doesn't dare. He waits till the doors to the ambulance are closed and allows himself to be led over to Richmond Street and a waiting car.

Before he gets in, he turns around and looks back. He can tell something isn't right. The ambulance pulls away very slowly and there's no siren wailing and no blue light flashing. He puts a hand in his pocket and wraps it around the keys. *What does that mean?*

But he already knows the answer.

He finds himself staring at the back of the ambulance and mouthing, 'Jack, come back.'

April 2015

Stuart fastens his belt and steps out of the clearing. As he exits the cruising ground, he becomes aware of footsteps behind him.

'Hang on, don't rush off!' someone shouts in a northern English accent.

Stuart turns around and is surprised to see the man he's just had sex with. 'Oh, hello,' he stammers. 'Where are you *from*?'

'Bradford,' replies the man, smirking.

'Sorry,' says Stuart, 'I had no idea.' He's worried he's

just said something racist – or that his assumption of the man's origins reveals a prejudice he wasn't even aware of having. 'I'm from Manchester,' he adds. 'Well, Blackburn originally.'

The man's smirk grows into a grin. 'I could tell you were a northerner from the way you said 'Fuck!' when you shot your load.'

Stuart finds himself laughing. 'Yeah, I do tend to do that.'

The man puts his hand in his pocket and takes out his vape. 'Don't apologise, it were hot.'

Stuart chuckles. He remembers that just as he was building up to climax, the man turned his head and kissed him. Without knowing why, Stuart found himself returning the man's kisses. That actually turned him on more.

He should get back to his cab but realises he wants to stay and talk to this man.

'I don't do much cruising these days,' he ventures. 'I'm getting on a bit, you know.'

The man lets out a plume of smoke. 'Me too, I'll be fifty next birthday. I don't have quite the same urge anymore.'

Stuart lets his smile creep into his eyes. 'Well, you seemed to have plenty of urge just then.'

The man leans back on the railings. 'I guess summat came over me when I saw you in t' caf eating your schnitzel.'

Stuart's eyebrows shoot up. 'Oh, I didn't see you in there. Sorry, I like keeping myself to myself.'

'Don't worry, same 'ere. Without stating t' obvious, it's one of t' reasons I do this job. Or at least it were. Lately, I've been getting a bit sick of my own company.'

Stuart nods.

There's a pause.

'Listen, I've got a kettle in me cab,' the man says, tucking his vape into his pocket. 'I don't suppose you fancy a brew?'

Stuart runs his hand over his stubble. 'Yeah, go on then.'

September 1984

It's the end of another night out and Stuart and Jack are walking back to Stuart's flat.

'I'm afraid it's t' usual deal,' Stuart says. 'You'll have to leave in t' morning before t' landlord gets wind. Sorry, I know it's a pain. But I'll come with you and we can get some brekkie.'

Jack shrugs. 'I'm hardly going to complain after what we heard tonight.'

Stuart feels a twist in his gut. 'I know what you mean.'

While they were in Stuffed Olives, Stuart and Jack heard that one of the bar's regulars has died. Nick is just the latest in what's becoming a long line of their friends or acquaintances to be taken by AIDS. Yet again they won't be invited to the funeral. Nick's family is holding it in Wales and they've made it clear his friends aren't welcome – or at least not the gay ones.

Jack folds his arms. 'Stu, are you frightened? About AIDS?'

Stuart lets out a breath. 'Yeah.'

'Me too.' Jack pauses. 'What if one of us has already got it?'

Stuart does his best to sound positive. 'Well, we're both fit and healthy, neither of us has got any symptoms and we're doing what they tell us – we just have to hold on to that. Until someone invents a test.'

Jack kicks a discarded can down the pavement. 'You know, if anything happens to me, I want you to move on.'

'What do you mean?'

'Just that if I die, I don't want you moping around for t' rest of your life. I want you to be 'appy. I want you to find someone new.' Jack reaches the can and gives it another kick. 'After an acceptable period of mourning, obviously.'

Stuart manages a weak smile. 'Give over, Jack. Stop talking daft.'

Jack unzips his coat and flips it back so it forms a cape over his shoulders. 'Stu, I'm serious! If I die I want you to spread your wings and keep flying!'

'Oh, pack it in! Nowt's going to happen to either of us!' Stuart slides in front of him and kicks the can before Jack has the chance. 'Now put your coat on properly and tell us about this walk in' t' Peak District.'

April 2015

Stuart walks around his truck, doing his checks. The lights are working, the registration plate is still attached to the trailer and the straps holding down the curtains are tight. There's no sign of any damage to the bodywork, mudguards or mirrors, and there are no rips, tears or cording on the tyres. The airlines from the cab to the trailer are properly connected and the kingpin is still attached.

Stuart climbs into his cab, takes off his gloves and enters the current time into the tacho. The message displayed changes to 'ready to drive'. He turns the key in the ignition and pulls the vehicle out of the lorry park.

As he re-joins the *autobahn*, his eyes flit from the road

onto the phone number that's written on a piece of paper resting on the dashboard. Above it is a name: *Hassan*.

In thirty years, Hassan is the first person Stuart's met who he thinks he'd like to see again. *And Jack did say I should move on. I expect he'd be annoyed at me for moping around all these years.*

But would I be able to?

In the sky ahead, a flock of swallows dances into view. They glide and swirl around each other, forming shapes that pulse in and out like a heart beating. *If it's spring they must be on their way back from Africa.*

Stuart picks up the piece of paper.

Yeah, I think I will call him.

He presses down on the accelerator.

Matt Cain is a writer, broadcaster, and a leading commentator on LGBTQ+ issues. His breakthrough novel, *The Madonna Of Bolton*, was published in 2018, followed by *The Secret Life of Albert Entwistle*, *Becoming Ted* and *One Love*. In 2024, his Quick Read *Game On* was one of the official short novels of World Book Night. In 2025, he was awarded an MBE for services to LGBTQ+ culture. Born in Bury and brought up in Bolton, Matt now lives in London with his husband, Harry, and their cat, Nelly.

Call Me Donna – George Parker

Eat me like you'd eat a kebab.
Two a.m., my juices running down your chin.
Get me while I'm hot.

Eat me like I'm your fucking donner.
Unwrap me, not fully. Just enough to work your
mouth
around my dripping flesh, your hands holding me
together,
clasped tight in prayer, circling my neck, force me
into your throat.

Eat me like I'm the kebab you were ravenous for at
half-past four
on the night bus, face puffed but happy, lit by
fleeting neon
and the memory of your Christ-like I-am-God
becoming on the dance floor.

As cigarette smoke-dawn spills past windowpane,
I want you to be picking me from between your teeth,

my odour a permanent stain on your skin,
and yes, your arsehole sore
from our consummation.

George Violet Parker is a Pushcart, Best of the Net, and Space Crone Prize-nominated queer disabled writer, performer and facilitator. Publications include collaborative pamphlet *Not Your Orlando* (Pink Dust) and *Twisted Roots* (Reconnecting Rainbows). Their debut collection *Gynandromorph* (Written Off) and ACE-funded anthology *effable* (fourteen poems) are recently published. Other writing has appeared in Mslexia, Financial Times, Arachne Press, Bi+ Lines, and more.

Self-Portrait As Fragment 31 – Han Smith

φαίνεταί μοι κῆνος ἴσος θέοισιν

They win because they are fleshed, grown trees already. They know their own strength and the way they are seen: this is how they win and break everything.

ἔμμεν' ὤνηρ, ὄττις ἐνάντιός τοι

My feet are bare. I never wear shoes here. Why would I?

ἰσδάνει καὶ πλάσιον ἆδυ φωνεί-

He is, in fact, a stranger, here only by chance, but his strength is something fully earthed and unstunted. He has roots here before him that are certain and solid. He is real and visible like any whole tree should be. And he happens to walk through this park: a pure stranger. He happens to take the path by the two of us in the blue shirts with the badges on them, spooling out a hose on a reel between new saplings. He happens to be passing, and then the next part must be choice. He stops. He comes closer to the two of us, or rather, to just the one. The one of the two in the cracked white sandals.

My feet are bare. I have a hand on the reel and the metal bend is warmed in the sun but not trusted, now. The heat can drain at any moment. My feet are bare and my fingers know this.

Any chance of a drop of that for me? says the stranger.

σας ὐπακούει

The one in cracked sandals looks to me, my feet bare, and then she looks to him. She says: The water's – it's really only meant for the trees.

Is it clean? says the stranger. Just a drop of it. That's all I need.

καὶ γελαίσας ἰμέροεν, τό μ' ἦ μὰν

I'm not sure, says the one in cracked sandals. If it's clean enough to drink, I mean.

It's not, I say, my feet bare. It comes from the river.

I'm waiting, my feet bare, for the face. I'm waiting for the face of the one in cracked sandals. The one in cracked sandals should be smiling now, even if the smile is a hiding, undercover one. It's better, even, if the smile is hiding, when the river – our crept river – is all a kind of hiding.

καρδίαν ἐν στήθεσιν ἐπτόαισεν·

The hiding smile does not come to the face. I wait, my feet bare: it will come. It still can.

ὠς γὰρ ἔς σ᾽ ἴδω βρόχἐ, ὤς με φώναι-

I'm not sure it is from the river, says the one in cracked white sandals. You know? It's attached to a cistern underground. I think it's clean.

It's safe then, to drink? the stranger says.

You'll just have to take my word for it, the one in cracked white sandals says.

And here there is a smile, but it is wrong. It is a mirror-trick, mockery warp of a smile. It is hiding, of a kind, but not the river-hiding kind. It is hiding but too obviously hiding, and smiling for the stranger, entirely. It is a hiding, impossibly, from me, my feet bare.

σ᾽ οὐδ᾽ ἒν ἔτ᾽ εἴκει,

The stranger says: I'll have to do just that. You work here, after all, don't you?

Yes, says the one in cracked sandals. Well, I don't know if—

Yes, I say, my feet bare. We work here and we live here, yes.

The one in white cracked sandals shrugs, and this too is for the stranger only. I don't know if it really counts as work, she says, and something she does with her eyes is uncaring. It's only for the summer and we're practically paid nothing, she says. But we get meals and the hut at the gates to stay in, and you never know when these watering skills might come in handy.

ἀλλ ἄκαν μὲν γλῶσσα ἔαγε, λέπτον

The one in cracked white sandals says this with her new smile and new shrug, and the eyes thing, and by saying and smiling and shrugging, she is ruining. By not saying, as well, she is ruining. When she says, We get meals, she does not say: We eat bread and garlic and rosemary, together, in the evenings on the outside bench and we flick the grey berries off that land on the table. When she says, The hut, she does not say: Our hut. What she does not say is fading flat by not saying.

δ αὔτικα χρῶι πῦρ ὐπαδεδρόμηκεν,

They certainly can come in handy, says the stranger. You never know who might turn up here thirsty, do you?

Fading is ruining and ruining is losing. The stranger is collapsing us without even seeing.

It isn't just the water for the trees, I say, my feet bare. Even if it's just for the summer, we actually have a lot to do. There's the herbs we grow and the vegetables, down at the far end, and there's picking up all the rubbish every morning. People leave their wrappers and bottles from their fun and we're the ones who clear it all up when it's done.

ὀππάτεσσι δ οὐδ ἒν ὄρημμ', ἐπιρρόμ-

I say this, my feet bare – my mouth says something like this – only for the one in cracked sandals to speak, too. She can save us and say: Yes. She can stop it from fading. She can say: And yes, when we pick up the bottles there's liquid to tip out and who knows what that filth is. We pour it like slime and it stinks but we have to, and it's fine because later the hose is for us. We spray each other clean and we shimmer. Or else we wash off in our crept river, when it's dark.

But the one in cracked sandals says none of this. And nothing of ripped mint leaves and *erba madre* between fingertips, nothing of first fat tomatoes bitten wet. It's only this weird thing for the summer, she says.

βεισι δ̓ ἄκουαι,

And you live in that hut? By the gates? says the stranger. Yes, says the one in cracked white sandals.

Our hut, I say, my feet bare.

Just the two of you? says the stranger.

Four of us, says the one in cracked sandals. They always have four here in the summer.

Four, says the stranger. So it must be quite a squeeze in there.

έκαδε μ' ἴδρως ψῦχρος κακχέεται, τρόμος δὲ

Four means nothing, and Squeeze means air. They come out as zeroes from his speaking and mean nothing. Four is not enough to mean: four bunks, four shelves, four badged shirts on the windowsill, and only one cupboard that also makes the kitchen wall. Four is not enough to be: the one in cracked sandals, the one with feet bare, the one scared of insects, and the one who makes the lemon cake. Four makes everyone the same and unfaced. Four is not the two who stay in with the radio, when two take the towels and cycle late to the riverbank.

παῖσαν ἄγρει, χλωροτέρα δὲ ποίας

Just girls, all of you, or what? says the stranger.

Just girls, says the one in cracked sandals, and this is the fading that ruins the most. Just girls is sound that is grotesque and does not match. A foot skimmed from a sandal, then out on river stones, is not Girls, but the Girls sound makes it Girls: makes it fade.

Well then, says the stranger.

Well, says the one in cracked sandals. Then?

Well, maybe I'll have to come by sometime to make sure you don't get too bored dead here, says the stranger.

Oh? says the one in cracked sandals and her voice is shaped to be surprised. Her eyebrows, and her head tilt, are surprised in this act-way. There is no true surprise in this inevitable fade now. That might be nice, she says. Why not.

It must get boring with just you four girls, I mean, says the stranger.

Not really, I say, my feet bare.

Sometimes, says the one in cracked sandals.

ἔμμι, τεθνάκην δ' ὀλίγω 'πιδεύης

So you can show me those herbs, or the vegetables, says the stranger. The way his mouth is next shows teeth, a mouth and teeth that are maddening to imagine open to taste pellet peas from a snap-pod. A thumbnail to slip the seam of the pod, then feed it to tongue, then raw fire under skin, in the heat of a field, feet bare in earth.

Tomorrow, says the stranger. Will you be here tomorrow?

We're always here, says the one in cracked sandals.

In the evening? he says.

Sure, she says.
Perfect, he says. The stranger says: Perfect.

φαίνομ' ἔμ' αὔται·

And yes, perfect, yes, and he is perfect, and right. He is nothing sealed, nothing locked or weak-withered. I'd better be off for now, he says.

But wait. He holds his hands close, out and cupped. I would like that drop first though, he says.

ἀλλὰ πὰν τόλματον ἐπεὶ καὶ πένητα

The one in cracked white sandals laughs. She is loud, and perfect also.

Of course, she says and she lifts the hose end: the hose that is meant for the sapling trees, with roots too small and shrunken and invisible to reach the water in the ground on their own, and the hose that is for shining two bodies bright. She holds it over his palms. Thick smack-fall of water. He drinks and she is watching him take what he knows without knowing he can claim and is entitled to.

She sees only his drinking and his upright, sure power, and only I, my feet bare, see the fading and draining. Slick water dashes from cupped hands onto boots, and they are safe, seen boots that will be by the hut door when I'm back from the riverbank, my feet bare, in the next days. I'll come back, my feet bare, alone and unshimmered, for the first time the only stripped skin in the current, and the one in cracked sandals will shrug and laugh and say that none of anything was real: it was just nothing. It was fun and dared and wild once but not real. And a sapling forgotten, meanwhile, never roots, because it fades and pales, for all that it burns.

Han Smith is a queer writer, translator and community literacy teacher. She received a London Writers Award in 2019/2020. Her debut novel *Portraits at the Palace of Creativity and Wrecking* was published by John Murray Originals in June 2024, and was shortlisted for the 2024 Goldsmiths Prize. Twitter/Instagram: @Han_Smiff; website: www.han--smith.com.

And I'll Scratch Yours – Wayne Berkeley Herbert

Gordon spaced mundane activities across each week to reduce voids of solitude. As a man in his mid-forties he'd given up on lightning bolts and settled for the occasional jolt.

It was Tuesday, which meant the Post Office. There was a small sub-branch in the London enclave he called home. It was rarely busy, and the postmistress was good for five-minutes of chatter. It was late September with a fresh chill in the air, which would provide an excellent lead into conversation about the onset of autumn.

It was time to hang up his linen coat. He grabbed a woollen sports jacket from the wardrobe in its stead and slipped it on. It wouldn't button across his gingham shirt and striped tie. He was aware his girth was expanding, but this was vexing. He made a mental note to stop having butter with afternoon tea.

After making himself as smart as possible he set off. His neighbour was in the front garden wrestling a forsythia. Mr White didn't acknowledge Gordon. It was inconsequential as they would share a coffee over the rear garden fence on Sunday morning. Gordon had already heard about the overgrown wild bush and would be able to ask whether its reduction had been a success.

'Good morning, Mrs McIntyre.' Gordon was pleased the Post Office was free of other customers. He opened the side pocket of his jacket and pulled out an envelope.

'Good morning, Mr Petlove. How can I help you?'

She didn't comment on the new seasonal attire. He tugged the two sides of the jacket together to appear fastened. 'First class postage for one letter please.' Gordon placed the package on the sliding metal tray.

Mrs McIntyre didn't react.

Gordon cleared his throat. 'The temperature drop has called for a thicker layer today.'

Mrs McIntyre nodded. 'Sixty-four pence please.'

He saw her register the addressee – Rupert Hildreth, his school friend. She'd remarked previously about the unswerving regularity of their correspondence. They'd written to each other bi-weekly since university. But on this occasion, she remained silent.

Gordon pressed on. 'I suspect it will soon be time for a scarf and—'

'I'm afraid I don't have the time today.'

Gordon couldn't believe the audacity but kept his own council.

'You can always buy stamps from the machine in future to save queuing.' Mrs McIntyre pointed to a red metallic hulk.

He counted exact change from a leather coin pouch, bid her good day and left. They had not fallen out as far as he was aware. Yes, they'd exchanged words about the state of the National Health Service last week and levels of unemployment the week before, but it was no worse than opposing politicians. He welcomed the debate. Perhaps the change in air pressure had made her cross.

Gordon closed the door behind him and froze. He didn't know what to do next. The lack of conversation had upset his equilibrium, and he didn't relish returning home to Radio 4. He wondered whether the more enthusiastic chatter on Radio 2 would make a difference, but he couldn't stomach their ghastly disc jockeys.

He would walk the long way home. He set off deflated and tried in vain to fasten his coat. A visit to John Lewis at the weekend was required for a larger size. This was no time to be starving himself of butter.

As he approached the green outside the town hall he pondered on whether he should visit the fishmongers, but he went to the fishmongers on Thursdays when they had a fresh delivery. A jar of fish soup was always useful for the larder, however, he reasoned.

'Good morning.' Gordon strode in.

'Yes. Hello. How can I help?' The aproned man emerged from the side of the display and stood next to the scales.

'You're probably wondering why I'm here today.' Gordon gazed at the display. The selection was reduced – as he thought it would be.

'Hmmm. What would you like? The mackerel is on special.' The fishmonger looked beyond Gordon. 'Good morning, Mrs Tilbury. I'll be with you shortly.'

'Do you want to serve the lady first while I decide?' There wasn't much Gordon desired other than soup and a chat.

'You're fine. I'm closing in a few minutes. We always take an early and longer lunch on Tuesday to prepare the smoker. Now how can I help?'

'Fish soup please.'

Gordon was hurried out without interaction other than the exchange of broth and coinage.

The additional expenditure meant that he was running lower on cash than he liked. He stopped at the cash-point – not daring to go back to the Post Office where he held an account. He hated using the plastic debit card but needs must.

'*Big Issue* mate?' The scruffy youth waggled a dog-eared magazine in Gordon's direction.

'Pardon me?' Gordon put the £20 note in his pocket.

'Do you want a copy of the *Big Issue* – helping the home-less?' The youth smiled.

'No. Thank you.' Gordon feared it was only the local homeless who wanted to engage with him.

'Come on. Give a guy a break will ya? What's wrong with everyone today?' The youth shuffled.

Gordon noticed the youth had an empty Maltesers bag stuck to his filthy trainers.

'OK, well if you don't want a mag, how about a note for some lunch?' He put his wares into a cheap plastic shoulder holdall.

'I've no idea what you're talking about.'

'The reddies mister.' He rubbed his fingers together.

A firm no should mean that, but the day was already out of kilter. Gordon looked at the street seller. He was un-kempt and needed a good wash but that didn't stop a cheeky grin shining through. And now he came to think it over he was flattered at the insistent attention. He'd admired the vitality of young men from afar but hadn't had the chance to be their sole interest.

'I didn't think you were permitted to ask for cash.'

'We're not . . . I'm desperate . . . Sorry.'

Gordon looked the young man square in the eyes and saw a loneliness he recognised all too well. He had to help, or he was no better than Mrs McIntyre or the fishmonger. 'In that case I can offer you a cup of tea and a toasted ham and cheese sandwich.'

'I'd prefer the dough.'

'Take it or leave it.' This was hopeless. Gordon wasn't sufficiently despairing to beg a beggar, and he walked on.

'Where would we go?'

'My home. It's only a few minutes' walk from The Broadway.' Gordon wondered if it was reckless to extend an invitation to an unknown and seemingly unsavoury character. However, if his routine was forcing changes on him, he'd make some changes himself and bugger the consequences.

'S'pose that would be OK. It's not like anyone's buying today.'

'Don't do me any favours.'

'I won't.'

They walked together without conversation. It was as if expectations had changed – like a date agreeing to go home with you for the first time – not that Gordon had been on dates.

'Not far now.' Gordon broke the silence.

'Do you often take people you meet on the street to your home?'

'No. I usually know their name.'

'Jim. Jimmy. Jimbo. James. Take your pick.'

'How do you do, James. Gordon.' He held out his hand.

'All right Gordo.' James grabbed Gordon's outstretched palm and shook it.

'It's Gordon.'

Gordon opened the gate. 'After you, James.' He was glad that Mr White was not to be seen. The forsythia looked hacked to death.

Gordon picked the mail from the mat. A quick glance told him that two of the three were marketing material and the third a bill. He placed them on the polished hallway table and hung up his jacket. 'Come in. Make yourself at home.' He regretted the latter as soon as the words left his lips.

James looked uncomfortable. 'Can I use the loo please?'

'Yes. Second door on the left.' Gordon maintained a calm expression but worried what was concealed beneath the coat.

During lunch James spoke of life lived from hostel to hostel, culminating on the streets. He didn't mention family and it would have been impolite to ask.

Gordon set his napkin on his knees. 'After being spotted in an Alan Ayckbourn play at the Palace Theatre in Watford I was cast in a major British film. A supporting role. Now what do you think of that James?'

'Wow. I thought you looked familiar.'

'That's unlikely to be ... The director, a temperamental soul at the best of times, didn't like suggestions for my character. He said that support roles were just that, and my two lines didn't warrant discussion.' Gordon sat back and folded his arms.

'Sounds like an arse to me.'

'He was. I said that I'd seen one line change the success of a production and this was a main support role.' Gordon paused. 'He had me removed from the set and followed through on his plan to make sure I didn't work again. I was dropped by my agent and couldn't even secure a job as an extra. And now I, I, I . . .'

'Glad you stuck up for your rights. It's about self-respect. We're in similar positions.' James rested his cutlery on the table. 'So how do you afford all this?

Gordon reddened. He was ashamed that all he'd ever amounted to was a modest income from his mother's estate. 'Cake? It's an iced Madeira.'

'Yeah. Great. Thanks. Haven't had anything like that since my gran . . .'

It seemed they both had plenty left unspoken.

James departed after cake. The visit had taken over two hours. It was the longest Gordon had spent with company in a long time. And he'd enjoyed sharing his acting tales. Sated, he took an afternoon nap in the conservatory.

Eggs.

He'd forgotten to buy them. It wasn't too late. Omelette would still be on the supper menu. He dashed out before the shops closed.

Standing in front of the cashier he searched again. Where was the £20 note?

What a fool.

There would be no omelette.

Gordon spent the next week dismissing negative thoughts from his mind. After all, he only had himself to blame. Fawning over a young man. Letting his guard down. He'd been naive.

Gordon didn't go to the Post Office. He'd decided to sever relations with Mrs McIntyre. He hoped that he'd find his new acquaintance in the same spot.

James jumped when he saw Gordon walking towards him.

'Ah, there you are James.'

'Oh. Yeah. Hello.' James didn't look up and fiddled with his holdall.

'How's your week? Profitable?'

'Look. I'm sorry I took it. I admit it. It was just—'

Gordon held his hand up. 'Are you available for lunch?'

There was a pause before James spoke. 'Errrr yes but I don't understand.'

'Good. I'll see you 1 p.m. promptly.' Gordon smiled and walked on.

The bell rang only a few minutes late.

'Come in, come in.' Gordon ushered James over the threshold. 'I've some fresh corned beef from the butcher. Now do you want to take a shower? I'll wash those clothes for you too. There's a robe and towel in the guest room.'

James stood still.

'Chop chop. We haven't got all day.' Gordon walked towards the kitchen. 'And James, there's an envelope addressed to you on the hallway table.' He didn't look back.

James collected his mail and closed the bedroom door.

Gordon had wondered whether he'd dare ask the young man to sit before him in a bath robe. Well, why not. It was nothing more salacious than that. And if he didn't want to he could take the money and flee.

Gordon felt more adventurous than he had in years. He needed to change and start living. Perhaps he'd thank Mrs

McIntyre for being the unwilling catalyst. But not today. There was tea to brew and sandwiches to garnish.

'James?' Gordon called out. 'Do you like English or French mustard with your beef?'

Wayne Berkeley Herbert is a Director of Hastings Book Festival and currently studying for a PhD in Creative Writing at the University of Brighton. He writes fiction in both short and novel lengths. When he is not writing you can usually find him walking the two best-looking cockerpoos in East Sussex on the beach.

How to Tell a Priest You're Queer – Anna Nightingale

first, avocado toast, as frank o'hara
so wisely decreed.
then, put your head beneath
the unblessed water,
& yes, the water is
almost as unclean as you are
& no, it's not your only baptism,
nor is it your fault.
dress yourself as an apology
but you are not apologising.
bring along your diaries
& show the father the lengths to which
you'd have gone
to ensure that burning was
not your future: tell him you'd have slaughtered
    every beast, swum through sand for forty
    nights,
forgotten to eat for good – whatever it took
to quell the flames. bring your rosaries

& your mother's & your mother's mother's
just in case. choose a pew at the front
to kneel at and wait your turn, shoulders back,
soft gaze, defiant.
enter the box. don't
sugar-coat it.
tell him how it feels to be touched
on the thigh – like a thousand angels
singing in your stomach. tell him
what you know of desire, how strange
and struggling a thing it is, like a snake
kept in a cracked glass box in the basement
of a house: writhing and unstoppable.
when he says nothing, take out
your dagger. put it not through his chest
but through the rope that binds you.
listen to yourself as you whisper
o, the ferocity of the free.

Anna Nightingale lives and writes in Coventry.

West End Wendy – Avi Ben-Zeev

PiggycubXL sends a 'woof' on Scruff, the hookup app for guys into hairy men. Taking the bait, I sink into the black-leather armchair and click on his profile. The man is looking for no-strings-attached sex or a friend with benefits. He's in an open relationship, enjoys Sunday roasts, rambling in the South Downs, and getting fucked by a pack of cigar-smoking leathermen, blindfolded.

I swipe left, not because there's anything wrong with PiggycubXL's looks or desires. Sexual freedom? Bring out the pom poms. It's just that I'm looking for love in all the wrong places. In London, like San Francisco, the gay male apps work dandy for hookups – the more specific, the better – but for dating, and dare I say it, romance, not so much.

Sure, I love waking up in blissful silence and making my coffee just the way I want it. Still, there's nothing quite like a tender-hearted, big-bellied bear who looks at me in that special way, you know, cheeks flushed, sparkling eyes. The urge to share our deepest secrets and laugh like hyenas, schoolboys, or both. And sex. Unabashed, kinky, connected sex that ends in sticky cuddles.

I don't owe PiggycubXL a response, but being ignored doesn't feel good, at least not to me. 'Appreciate the woof, but I'm looking to date atm. Happy hunting!'

'Too bad,' PiggycubXL texts back, the flashing dots indicating he's not quite done. 'Do you have a pussy?'

'No, I like dogs,' I type.

'I meant vagina,' he clarifies, as though I didn't get it the first time around.

More than two decades into gender transition, my idealised self wouldn't give a shit, but my actual self does.

In the early days, the thought of sex with a non-trans man mortified me. 'Why set myself up to be rejected?' I asked Jon, my San Francisco therapist. It was a rhetorical question, but Jon wouldn't have any of it.

'How a guy reacts to your genitals has everything to do with him and nothing to do with you. You know that, right?' he exclaimed, grazing his chin stubble.

I tried protesting, 'Yes, but—'

'No buts. Just do it,' Jon insisted.

He was right (like he always was), and, sure, I've experienced trans panic moments over the years – guys who froze at the thought of my down there – but those pale in comparison to the many hot and tender moments I've shared with beautiful non-trans queer men I've dated and fucked.

Besides, I'm lucky to be trans. We're a gloriously diverse bunch, engaging with life with the kind of curiosity and freedom only journeying home brings.

So, when it comes to why I'm single, truth be told, it's me who's become overly picky. Is intimacy something I even . . . Wait, a woof from West End Wendy? Well, hello, handsome!

Sitting upright, I click on West End Wendy's profile with that familiar foolish hope. Hell, you never know.

Turns out, like me, he's in his fifties; a nice change from the younger men looking for a daddy. His smile is more capybara than bear, and I mean it as a compliment. Truly. Those large rodents are endearing. And what do you know, the guy's looking for friends with benefits or a relationship.

It gets better. West End Wendy plays the piano, likes West End shows and experimental theatre, and bakes. If he makes a mean Eton Mess, then be still, my heart.

'How are you?' he messages before I get a chance to woof back.

'Doomscrolling when I should be writing or going on a London adventure.'

'Goodness gracious, a conversation instead of a dick pic,' he types, inserting a winky emoji. 'May I ask what you're writing?'

'My memoir,' I respond, cringing at how pretentious that sounds.

'Fascinating. Tell me more.'

'Well, it's a love-hate story between a gay man and his straight female past.'

'I'd be delighted to hear all about it. Five o'clock teatime tomorrow in the West End? I'll have forty minutes to spare if that's OK.'

'Sure,' my fingers type with a will of their own. The guy seems promising, yes, but tomorrow feels rushed, and besides, it's been a while since I've made plans for a date, date on Scruff. For more relationship-oriented meetups, I've switched to Hinge, as the guys on there seem to want more than a wham-bam. It was Pete Buttigieg, the former US presidential candidate, who made Hinge famous by meeting his husband, Chasten, on that site. Since then, it's become the go-to for gay men searching for strings online.

In the past month alone, I've gone on eight Hinge dates. The French Doctor. The Jewish Doctor. The German Vegan. Tortured Artist. The Man with the Curl. Cross-stitching trans4trans guy. Sober Fashionista. And last but not least, Standup Comic, who I couldn't wait to take home after a passionate make out in an alley, but when he took off his pants, the stench was . . . No, why replay the sordid details? But seriously, wiping one's ass shouldn't be optional. And now, at number nine, comes West End Wendy with the promise that maybe, just maybe, the pain of dating might just pay off.

I swear I tried my best not to be early for the date, but damn it, it's 4.45 p.m., and here I am outside Leicester Square station walking into the hustle and bustle – hordes of tourists milling about, taking selfies, planting themselves in the middle of sidewalks, and worse, stopping at red lights when they should be throwing themselves against traffic or risk creating a sidewalk jam.

It wouldn't hurt to be more empathetic. When I first arrived in this city, I misguidedly thought that jaywalking was wrong and I had not yet perfected the locals' walk-meets-run while muttering *sorry, sorry, sorry*, which translated into British English means, get the fuck out of my way.

Wait, is that . . .? Yes. I spot Wendy across the street, pacing back and forth in front of the café, the wind whipping his dachshund-patterned scarf around his face.

I smile as I approach. 'Hi, it's me, Avi.'

'Hurray,' he says, taking both my hands and giving them a gentle squeeze. 'Hurray.' He's more handsome in person – hazel eyes with large specks of green and that winsome capybara grin.

Inside, the place is buzzing with after-work professionals in business casual and pre-pre-theatre dinner-goers in shades of black. In the US, a place this crammed would be loud, but here people's tones are hushed and blend into the architecture – exposed brick walls softened by ambient lighting, offsetting the lingering grey outside.

As luck would have it, we snag a table and order two flat whites from an uncharacteristically cheerful waitress.

'So, tell me more about your book.' Wendy fishes a stick sachet from the sugar packet holder, hovers it over his cup, and tears it in the middle.

'I've never done it this way,' I say, mesmerised by the efficiency. 'I always tear off the tip.'

'Well, I dare say you're in good company. It is rumoured that the sugar stick inventor killed himself because people didn't understand how to use it properly.'

'Now, that's an uplifting story.'

Wendy grins. 'I aim to please in more ways than one.'

'Is that so?' I revert to a playful tone.

'Yes, Sir!' he lowers his eyes for a moment, then gazes at me again. 'So, your memoir, how far back does it go?'

'The first and third parts focus on me, Avi. The part sandwiched in between is about her, Talia, my—'

'I see nothing but sexy man when I look at you,' he blurts out.

I'll take sexy, especially as I'm getting older and less secure in my attractiveness, but the man bit, what else should I look like?

My silence must have unnerved him because he adds, 'Dressed, obviously.' And when I still can't find the right words, Wendy utters, 'But I've always said that my brain is my primary sex organ.'

He means well. I see that, I really do, but it's high time to pivot. 'So, what exciting plans do you have this evening?' I ask.

'Dinner and a show with an American friend. A dreadful musical, really. But my friend wants to go, so what can you do?' He mock rolls his eyes.

'What show—?'

'I'm rubbish at this dating business. You see, I was married for twenty-five years, and he passed a year ago.' There's panic in Wendy's voice.

'What a huge loss.' I place my palm on his. 'I'm sorry.'

'I must go, I'm afraid.' My date gets up. 'But I want to see you again.'

'I'd like that,' I say. Awkwardness and all, we've barely scratched the surface.

Wendy whips out his phone. 'How about dinner Saturday? My place?'

'Homemade dessert?'

'Tell me what you'd like, and I'll make it.'

So, really, how could I say no?

Muswell Hill is an affluent, villagey London neighbourhood. The streets are lined with cherry trees and sycamores, and the red-brick houses are unconcerned with London's latest architectural trends. I can see how Wendy fits in with his Received Pronunciation – drawn-out 'a' sounds and 't's' that explode off the tongue.

I'm early. Again. But no way am I knocking on his door quite yet. Besides, how cool to explore. Turning the corner, a mom-and-pop cheese store appears in view, with a curved blue-and-pearl-oyster checkered façade. Ah, the perfect treat to go with my bottle of Rioja.

The shopkeeper, a lanky fellow with a wispy moustache, explains the concept of cheese in the way one talks to a toddler. 'Cheddar is not the only flavour, you see,' he adds, reacting to what exactly, my American accent? Tattoos?

'May I please taste the Gouda with cumin?' I ask, willing my brain to shut up.

'Certainly, Sir.' The man hands me a yellow cube freckled with seeds. For a moment, there's only the creamy nuttiness on my tongue, but the ping of an incoming text spoils it.

'I see you.' Damn, is Wendy here?

A knock on the windowsill, and there's my date, waving, in a shirt with a pelican print.

'Hi, handsome,' I say as I step outside. 'Sorry, I'm so annoyingly early.'

'Don't be silly.' He sets down a Waitrose bag filled to the gills and opens his arms.

We're the same age, so why do I feel like I'm hugging a much older man? And what's up with my ageism anyway?

'Shall we?' Wendy picks up his bounty and threads his free arm in mine. 'I hope you're hungry.'

His house is a two-storey Edwardian, ivy surrounding the bay windows. 'Welcome to my humble abode,' he says as we walk through a Chartwell-green door into a brightly lit hallway.

'Shoes off?' I ask.

'Is London dirty?' Wendy takes off his coat and loafers. I follow suit, my black leather boots touching his brown suede shoes.

'Follow me,' he motions, and we walk past a living room with navy-blue walls, a grand piano and dark wood furnishings and into a spacious black-red-and-white kitchen.

'What a beautiful home,' I say, uncomfortable about being uncomfortable.

'I remodelled after Stephen died.'

'Ah,' I utter, curious about what the place looked like before.

Wendy places the Waitrose bag on the marble counter. 'Keep me company while I finish cooking?'

'Sure,' I say, sitting at what looks like a 50s diner set. The placemats are laminated black-and-white photos of a couple walking on a beach, arm in arm – Wendy and a sandy-haired guy with an ocean-wide smile.

As someone who doesn't cook – I know, I know, but Mom's dishes were, well, how can I say it without offending the dead? . . . somewhat traumatic – I melt when someone prepares food from scratch. And Wendy has made a feast. Sweet and crispy prunes wrapped in bacon as appetisers. Roast chicken with honey mustard parsnips and carrots for the main. (Who knew parsnips could be so delicious?)

So, yeah, the food is tasty, but our conversation has been underwhelming at best. It's like Wendy checked out after serving the appetisers.

'So, where did you say you grew up?' I pick up where we left off.

Wendy dabs the corners of his mouth with a white linen napkin. 'Yorkshire, and you?'

'Tel Aviv, but I escaped from my fascistic country as soon as I could.'

'I see. More parsnips?'

'Yes, please. Delicious.'

'Why thank you, I bought them at the farmer's market.'

I pride myself on being able to hold a conversation, but not this time. When dessert rolls by, we give up, eating our sticky toffee pudding in silence. It's weird to be this quiet on a date, but out of thin air a Siamese cat jumps on the seat next to Wendy and gives me a *what gives?* kind of stare, breaking the lull.

'And you are?' I ask, intrigued by the creature.

'That's Judy, Stephen's cat,' Wendy says.

Judy meows at the sound of her name or maybe at Stephen's. 'For heaven's sake, it's not dinner yet.' Wendy gives Judy a stern look. 'He spoiled you, didn't he?'

'So, you don't think of her as yours, then?'

'Well, I'm not a pet person, but Stephen made me promise I'd take good care of Judy. Last thing he said before they wheeled him into the operating theatre.'

I'm no cat expert, but I'm moved to say something affirming. 'She looks happy.'

'You Americans are obsessed with being happy. Us, English, are wed to our gloominess.' Wendy scratches Judy's chin, and the cat purrs and arches her back.

'True, "Have a nice day" gets oppressive.'

Wendy's capybara smile is back. 'You didn't leave much on your plate. I take that as a good sign.'

'You should. Everything was so, so good. Thank you.'

'My pleasure.' Wendy clears our table. 'I realise I haven't been much fun, but tomorrow is the anniversary of Stephen's death, you see.'

It's considerate of him to explain, and, of course, now it all makes sense.

'What was he like?' I ask.

'Stephen? Well, he was different from me. He was kind,' Wendy mutters, loading the dishwasher. 'Why don't you relax in the living room while I finish cleaning up.' He's tearing up, I can see that, and my gut says to hug him, but touch has different rules here. Besides, we're still new to each other, Wendy and me, and he might not want a hug.

The living room screams old-school gay man: a Judy Garland throw pillow, curated on the brown-leather Chesterfield just so, a vintage poster of *La Cage aux Folles* in a gilded frame, and mahogany floor-to-ceiling bookshelves populated with classic tomes; authors like James Baldwin, Christopher Isherwood, Walt Whitman, Oscar Wilde and Tennessee Williams to name a few. And on the piano is a framed photo of the same man with the beautiful smile.

Unlike Wendy, I don't know what it's like to grow up as a queer boy, worship at the altar of gay male icons, or survive the AIDS epidemic. Attraction to men is one thing, shared history is another. It's like being an immigrant to my sexuality.

Mind on overdrive, I snag a Tom of Finland illustration book from the coffee table and sprawl on the Chesterfield. Tom and his playmates are the perfect escapist fantasy – chiselled faces, broad shoulders, thirteen-inch hard-ons bulging from leather pants and Double-D pecs. A hyper-masculinity so extreme, it's deliciously drag.

Wendy catches me fixated on a cop-cowboy duo. 'Camp at its best,' he says, laying a tray with two glasses and a bottle of tawny port on the coffee table and joining me on the sofa.

'Hi,' I say, noting the red in his eyes.

'May I kiss you?' Wendy pries Tom and company away from my clutch.

Leaning in, I let go into his gasp, the softness of his lips.

'Thank you,' Wendy says, as though I'm doing him a favour, or is he just being British? 'Speaking of kink,' he gestures at Tom, 'In your Scruff profile, you said you were dominant.'

'I can be, but only after I get to know a guy.' He's jumping the gun, and besides, I also wrote that I was looking for meaningful connections, so slow down, buddy boy.

'Spank me, Sir.' Wendy's cheeks are tomato red.

'Topping from the bottom?' I try for a light-hearted tone.

'So sorry.' He looks horrified. 'Please, spank me, Sir, I beg you. I cannot stand the pain.'

'You're grieving, I get that—'

'Please, Sir. Hard.'

I could become Sir and go into play mode. Make him beg some more, redden his bottom, no damage, of course, just the right sting to unclog the emotional well within. Switch from Sir to Daddy, and bring him to catharsis, a container to his tears. Hold him for as long as he needs.

My younger selves whisper, *Why not? Help the man feel and have fun while you're at it.* Resisting, I place my hand on Wendy's shoulder. 'I'm kinky, yes, but right now, I want to be wanted as me, Avi, not a role-play character. Does that make sense?'

'OK, vanilla sex then, but CMNM?'

I've seen that acronym on the apps, but I check to make sure. 'You mean, Clothed Man Naked Man?'

'Yes. I'll get naked for you, but I don't know how I feel about, you know, seeing your . . .'

'Good night,' I say, getting up.

'We haven't touched the port.' Wendy's voice is shrill. 'Please, I could really use the company.'

Would you love me if I gave you what you want? My younger selves are louder now, contorting into Wendy's needs, confusing desire with validation. I'm mad at them, mad at myself, for being weak, but Jon's voice chimes in too, more West Coast than Drill Sergeant this time: *The heart has infinite space.*

'Sorry for your loss,' I say, injecting warmth into goodbye.

Avi Ben-Zeev is a London-based gay trans man, high school failure and Yale PhD. A psychologist and author, he writes about identity, belonging, and home. His story, Angel, won the UK's first transgender writing competition, and his co-edited anthology, *Trans Homo,* was a Lambda Literary Award Finalist. His memoir *Calling My Deadname Home* has been longlisted for the 2025 Polari Prize. www.avibenzeev.com

No Hot Ashes – JP Seabright

I crack myself open with the ring-pull of hope, half a blister pack of anticipation, a small tube of lube thirsting in my back pocket, hit the streets of Dalston with its sudden sting of dogshit in the nostrils, the smear of fried chicken kissed across my cheeks, my lips smacking themselves to the beat of the damp bag of tinnies banging against my thigh, and I am ready, prised open with lust like a lightning conductor sparking down my spine, electricity flowing from my fingers, I need to earth myself in you, plant myself deep, fist first, tongue thirst, brace for impact, I'm lit like every streetlight from here to Shacklewell, strung like a pair of Nikes lobbed across a pylon, rumbling like rail lines under our feet, shaking through your body, like the way your fingers run rivers through my hair, the contour of my coccyx grinds the wall of the Superstore, mirroring the corrugation of the mattress on your floor, and the streets of the east are a cracked mirror

littered with coke and hope and chapsticks and
chopsticks, and we are all running free as the
foxes, fucking behind the bins, howling out
the night, see the pulse of desire dancing in
our necks, you can feel it too yeah?

JP Seabright (she/they) is a queer disabled writer living in London. They have six solo pamphlets published and four collaborations, encompassing poetry, prose and experimental work. They have been nominated for Pushcart Prize, Best of the Net, Forward Prize, and shortlisted (twice) for a Saboteur Award for Best Collaborative Work. More info at https://jpseabright.com

Illicit – Holly Edwards

The skyline to the south of Edinburgh is full of high drama, dominated by the gothic peak of Arthur's Seat and the jagged teeth of Salisbury Crags. But the howling wind and horizontal rain meant that Pete didn't look up as he arrived each day for work beneath the mountain, in the soulless estate that is Pollock Halls, the catered student halls of residence for undergraduates at the University of Edinburgh. The cluster of nineteen seventies-style tower blocks contrast horribly with the majesty of the hill, and in the middle is the ugliest of them all, the John McIntyre Centre, within which the thousands of residents have breakfast and dinner, although, student life being what it is, there are smaller crowds at breakfast than dinner.

At nineteen, Pete was the youngest of the catering team. He worked in the pot wash alongside the wiry, grey-haired Edna and Rabbie, a sullen, stooped bombsite of a man. Rabbie said very little and always had the sour, stale smell of the drink about him. Pete suspected Rabbie took a nip to get him through, but he hid it from Bridie, the hard-faced matriarch who ran the shift. Everyone feared and loved Bridie in equal measure; even the chefs, a rag tag, yellow-eyed bunch of sweat-stinking misogynists, were nice to her.

The pot wash staff came on shift first, finished last, stayed in their corner, spoke to nobody. They loaded the pot wash, pulled the hood down and pressed the button. *Unload, scrub the pans, take the rubbish, mop the floor, load the pot wash, pull down the hood, press the button, unload, clean the spillages, replenish the crockery, load the pot wash, pull down the hood, press the button, unload.* The chefs treated them like slaves, the dinner ladies talked to them like children, and to the moneyed students who ate in the hall they were as invisible as ghosts.

'Pete!' Edna's piercing voice carried over the shouting of the chefs, the whir of the fans and the ovens, the clatter of pots and pans, and Pete would come running to do whatever back-breaking, disgusting job she had lined up for him, his grey hat pulled down over his crew cut. Scrub the still-warm walk-in ovens clean of caked-on cheese from hundreds of traybake pizzas? On it. Clean the bin hatch, open to the elements on one side, down on his knees in the stinking, freezing space, hands red raw? Nae bother. Pete worked hard, took instruction well and had learned early in life not to complain.

When the dining room closed at nine, the catering team sat down to their meal. They got whatever was left, and by that time of night nobody had a mind to be picky, least of all a growing lad like Pete who piled his plate high. Speed was of the essence: the team got twenty minutes for their break and Bridie timed them, setting her watch in front of her at the table, calling out regular time-checks with her mouth full. There was a dead-eyed determination because food was all very well, but what everyone really wanted was a smoke. As soon as their plates were empty the team gathered in the cold outside, inhaling B&H king size, lighting a second one on the tip of the first.

The last day of term was always frantic. Rabbie only had one speed, so Pete stepped up his own pace and mostly had things under control when he was summoned by Edna's screech to clear up a breakage out front.

When he returned, it took him a moment to register the scene which met him. Christmas carols were blaring out across the dining room and the atmosphere had been festive, so for the briefest of moments Pete thought it had snowed in the pot wash. Rabbie was leaning against the hood of the machine, defeated, and as he cast his glassy eyes over Pete the illusion was broken. Soap suds were pouring out of the machine and billowing onto the floor like lava. Rabbie slammed his hand against the hood in anger.

'Fuck it!' he yelled. Among the chemical smell of the suds, the sour, rotting stench from the bins and the sweet, steamy odours of a thousand turkey dinners there was another perfume, sharp and tangy, the smell of Christmas spirit, and its source was this sodden wreck of a man. Rabbie swayed slightly, steadying himself on a stainless-steel shelf.

'What in the name of the man and the woman is this?' hissed Edna, who stood behind Pete surveying the devastation. In his drunkenness Rabbie had used the wrong chemicals, clogging up the pot wash with the clouds of suds. There was a brief window of silence as Edna filled her lungs, then 'BRIDIE!!!'

Pete winced, anticipating the hurricane of abuse that Bridie would bring but as she rounded the corner like a cyclone, she suddenly softened. The pot wash had stopped belching out suds and sat sadly dripping; both it and Rabbie were defeated, their lights gone out. 'What have you done, you bampot?' scolded Bridie, but there was no malice in her voice. Rabbie allowed himself to be talked to like a child; he'd been drunk on shift before, and they all knew he wouldn't be back after the holidays.

The rest of the shift was hard graft, as without the machine Pete had to wash every dish by hand. Edna helped as much as she could, but they were already short staffed and the festive atmosphere meant that the dining hall didn't empty until almost ten o'clock. It was gone eleven when Pete finally shrugged on his coat, wishing Merry Christmas to the team as they prepared to go their separate ways for the holidays.

Outside a thin, freezing rain was falling. Pete huddled under the guttering by the back door and lit a cigarette, the flame briefly illuminating his thin, sallow face. As he smoked, he looked up at the block in front of him, a seven-storey tower which housed around a hundred and fifty students. Most of the windows were dark; the student union would be doing a roaring trade. However as he watched, a window on the first floor lit up, framing a blond young man in a white T shirt. In one fluid movement the blond peeled off the T-shirt, revealing an evenly tanned, muscular torso. He disappeared from view for a second, before moving back to the window and putting on a pale pink shirt. The young man faced outwards, using his reflection in the window as a mirror to style his hair, and then stepped out of sight. Moments later the light went out.

Pete waited, a smudge of pale skin in the shadows. He smoked his cigarette to the butt, flicking it into the wet undergrowth. Staring into the dark, the image of the topless blond replayed in his mind. Some minutes passed before the front door of the tower block opened and the blond student emerged, wearing a brown woollen blazer over his shirt, with a black scarf around his neck against the cold. He stood looking out at the drizzle, before running off into the night. Once he was out of sight, Pete pulled his own thin coat around him. It was too late for a bus now, so he began the long walk home.

Christmas was the usual. His maw got a turkey crown from Scotmid and his da came round for the day. They played happy families, pulling crackers and having a laugh, but he kept a close eye on the empty cans of Tennent's in the kitchen bin, relieved when his maw fell asleep in front of the *Strictly* Christmas special before a row could kick off.

He went to CC Blooms with his mates on New Year, the sticky-floored jewel in Edinburgh's queer crown. It was packed out; most of the crowd were off their tits. Pete dropped a half at eleven, so he was nicely fizzing by the bells. He spent most of the night dancing but had a kiss and a wee fumble with a lad from the Borders called Greg. One of Greg's mates had the look of the blond in the window, but it wasn't him, and anyway he didn't look twice at Pete.

The second week of January Pete was back in the kitchen. At first he was on his own, but at least the machine was working again. By the end of the week however, Edna's daughter, a skinny wee thing with spiked bleach-blonde hair and milk bottle glasses named Sharon came to help out. She was moody at first, but on Tuesday night Pete went dancing at Vice and caught sight of Sharon across the room. She raised her Archers and lemonade in a salute, and Pete gave her a nod. They then lost each other in the pulsating lights, and when he saw her again, she was getting off with a girl with dyed black hair and DM Boots, their torsos pressed against each other while their feet tapped to the beat of the music.

Back at work, misreading their new friendship, Edna feared her daughter was soft on Pete and decided that the two shouldn't spend too long alone together. When she was Sharon's age, she already had the bairn at home, and she wanted better for her little girl.

'You're out front,' she announced to Pete. 'Stand by the desserts; they're allowed one each, but they'll try for two.'

Initially, Pete struggled to make himself seen. 'Just the one dessert, pal,' he'd say quietly, but the students were used to the more fearsome Edna who could make someone drop their smuggled sponge and custard with one raised eyebrow. Pete, with his skinny shoulders hunched and his hat pulled low over his eyes, was a soft target.

'You need to be more assertive, hen,' advised one of the dinner ladies. 'Show them who's boss. If Bridie sees how many are getting away with two desserts, she'll have your head.'

The next time someone tried to take two puddings he barked, 'Oi! One each!' with just the right level of menace behind his words. The culprit flinched in fright, and mumbling an apology replaced the bowl on the shelf. 'Good lad,' said Pete. This success boosted his confidence and after a while he began to enjoy the sense of power, inspecting each student's tray for illicit treats.

And suddenly there he was: the blond from the window. Close up he really was stunning: gently ruffled hair like a young Prince William, full, pink lips with a cupid's bow so defined it looked like it had been drawn with a sharpie, and a strong, square jaw. When he opened his mouth, his teeth were large, bright white and utterly straight. He was tall, about an inch taller than Pete, and broad. His faded pink Ralph Lauren polo shirt skimmed his pecs, the collar turned up as if he had just thrown his clothes on before leaving his room. Pete was so caught up in the image of this Adonis shrugging on his shirt that he almost missed a tray creeping by laden with extras.

'Put it back!' Snapping back to reality he yelled a little too loudly, and the student in question went white, sheepishly returning their stolen pudding. Pete was still scowling at him, when a voice close by gave him a start.

'Mate.' The blond student was standing right next to him, leaning in to make sure that only Pete could hear him. 'Mate, listen, I've been on an epic walk, and I'm starved. Could I please, just this once?' He gestured to his tray, a second bowl of pudding hidden under his napkin. He was standing so close to Pete that the two were almost touching.

'Aye, well, it's against the rules,' said Pete, but he was smirking, 'but since you said please.' He gave a brief nod, and the blond beamed, showing all his teeth.

'Top bloke!' he said. His voice was syrupy and self-assured, used to getting its own way.

This was the start of it. Edna saw that Pete had a knack for maintaining dessert discipline and so put him out the front again. Pete held the line and the students realised he was as tough as Edna. But the blond would catch his eye and sometimes give Pete a wink which sent a jolt of desire straight between his legs, and each day Pete would look the other way as the blond loaded his tray with contraband.

Aside from that first time, they never exchanged a word, not in the dining hall, nor in the erotically charged world of Pete's imagination. Whenever he got lucky on a night out, it was the blond's perfect pink pout that Pete pictured kissing. Watching a one-night stand undress, Pete would secretly score him against that mental polaroid of the blond in the window even though, if Pete was honest, he was one of hundreds, young men who all looked like they had hatched from the same clutch of Fabergé eggs. They wore the same polo shirts, they spoke with the same upper-class drawl. They drank cosmos at PoNaNa's or Why Not, they went skiing in Italy, they spoke to the dinner ladies with a mixture of condescension and contempt. Truth be told, Pete hated the lot of them; he relished catching them trying to sneak an extra crumble past him, the only time he would ever have the upper hand over these silver-spooned shites.

Easter approached. Pete and Sharon became sort of friends, partly because there weren't that many gay bars in Edinburgh, so they often found themselves gurning away side by side on the sweaty dance floor at CC's, but mostly because Pete discovered Sharon was always able to get ecstasy at short notice. Edna, although mostly oblivious to what Sharon got up to and who she got up to it with, nevertheless decided that Pete posed no threat to her daughter's honour and went back to dessert duty, so Pete was once again back in the pot wash.

Pete missed seeing the blond, but it was fun kidding around with Sharon. He took the opportunity to replenish the cutlery out the front whenever he could, hoping to catch sight of him, but no luck. The shift was extra busy, and soon he was lost in the endless drudgery, his face soaked from the steam and the skin on his hands puce from the heat of the pot wash. He got called 'soft lad' by one of the chefs because he didn't move out the way fast enough and got splashed with hot soup, but this was soon washed off when

Sharon opened the machine too early, drenching them both in scalding hot water: the usual shenanigans.

'Pub?' asked Sharon at the end of the shift, and he shrugged in agreement. 'I've got to do my time sheet, give me five,' she said, so he grabbed his coat and wandered out to sit on a bench. The biting cold of the winter had retreated, and there was a freshness in the late evening air that felt a bit like spring. As he smoked, he heard footsteps and looked up to see the blond approaching him. He looked dazed, as if he had just been punched. He was staring down at his feet, humming tunelessly and staggering a bit from side to side. Pete realised he was drunk.

'Heeeeey!' Looking up, the blond locked eyes with Pete, and his face lit up into a smile. 'It's dessert guy!' He plopped himself down onto the bench next to him, casually throwing his arm round Pete's shoulder. He felt warm and solid. His thumb brushed the back of Pete's neck in passing; the patch of skin where contact had been made felt to Pete like it was on fire. 'Mate, I'm wasted.'

'Aye, so it seems,' replied Pete, his voice steady. He stared straight ahead, not trusting himself to look round. 'You've had a skinful.'

The blond leaned back and closed his eyes. Pete glanced in his direction. In the orange light of the streetlamp his winter tan burned bright. The distance between their two mouths was little more than a hand span; a simple rearrangement of his weight and their lips would touch.

'Who's your mate?' Sharon's tinny voice broke the spell. She was smoking a cigarette which she held between her index finger and thumb, looking down on Pete and the blond.

'This is my main man!' said the blond, suddenly

animated, his eyes snapping open. 'He always lets me get an extra dessert. He's the best.' At this the blond leant over and planted a kiss on Pete's forehead, before getting unsteadily to his feet. 'You're a funny-looking bloke,' he added quizzically to Sharon, taking in her cargo pants and biker jacket before ruffling her hair.

'I'm a girl, you twat,' she spat back. The blond made an exaggerated show of being sorry.

'Oops, sorry mate. I'm so wasted.' He winked at Pete and then staggered back to his dorm. Pete watched him go, feeling equal parts desire and disgust.

'Is that your type?' she asked, incredulously. Pete cleared his throat and laughed.

'Nah, not really. He's fit though, I wouldnae say no.'

'Aye, well, he's a prick.' Sharon ground her cigarette under her heel. 'Come on, there's a bus in a bit. It's karaoke at Havana tonight, should be a laugh.'

Pete said nothing but got to his feet and followed Sharon towards the bus stop. Behind them loomed the mountain, and before them lay the night, just like always.

Holly Edwards graduated from the University of Edinburgh in 2002 and spent the next decade working in the hospitality industry before realising what she really wanted was a captive audience and so trained as a secondary school teacher. She is studying for an MA in Creative Writing and lives in East London with her wife.

My Gernika (or, #3: Asier) – Jon Russell Herring

Wednesday 13 April 1994

He meets me off the train at Gernika. It's cold for late spring in Spain, and Asier's wearing black jeans and a leather coat. He's also holding a half-baguette wrapped in tinfoil: I hear it scrunch as we hug. We try speaking in Basque as we walk through the town, even though I've only been learning it a few months, and his brown eyes are as warm and penetrating as I remember from our one, brief meeting at a friend's flat half a year ago. I feel excited about why he's invited me here today.

People greet him as we pass in the street, most of them our parents' age – Gernika is a small town. Asier whispers that one of them is his family priest. I can't help but sense the presence of the 1937 Luftwaffe bombardment around me, although I don't mention Picasso or *Guernica* or anything like that as I feel it'd be a bit obvious or weird. Then he leads me to the famous tree anyway, and I get a jolt of affection seeing how proud it makes him. I take a photo of it, which Asier refuses to be in.

'You didn't tell your flatmates you were meeting me today, did you?'

I shake my head, but I have told Rosana, because I just needed one other person to know where I am today, meeting an almost-stranger far from home for – for what?

At his grandmother's flat, Asier hands me the baguette. He unlocks the door and holds it with his arm stretched up high. I pass underneath and make a disloyal mental note to check the labels on the mailboxes in the hallway when I leave, because he's refused to tell me his surname.

He takes down a dark-patinaed coffee pot, fills it and sets it to boil. It's very quiet in the flat, and in the block around us too, but I don't feel scared. I sit on the kitchen table, swinging my legs. He walks over, closes his eyes, kisses me.

Next door, I'm surprised that the mattress is stripped bare, because the rest of the room looks quite lived in. On the bedside table, a Juan Goytisolo novel is splayed open, there's a box of tissues, a framed picture. On the wall above the bed there's an old clock with just the numbers 3, 6, 9 and 12. I'm wondering if Asier has done this before, but it's me who starts undressing first. Our jeans entwine and our belts clink as they drop onto the tiled floor.

He's so beautiful. We kiss and we kiss until his stubble makes my mouth sore, and I can feel his saliva in my beard. He smells of *agua de lavanda* and as I pull off the last of his clothes, he claims he's pale because it's early in the year, but to me his skin is golden all over.

I'm distracted by a memory of Laurent, the French assistant at college, telling a room full of second years: 'Of course, one can never call oneself truly bilingual until one has made love with a native speaker.' I am laughing while licking Asier's armpits and wondering, can I ask him if this is making me bilingual in Spanish or Basque, or both, but now I'm worried I'm starting to lose my hard-on because Laurent was so odious and self-satisfied.

'Jon, will you fuck me?' he says quietly. I start planning sentences in Spanish about how I didn't buy any condoms and how worried I am that this isn't going to be what he wanted and how difficult it might be, for him at least, to reach a satisfactory conclusion given my lack of experience.

But it's fine, and we're doing it and it's going well, really well. He gasps and grabs me really roughly, and I'm biting his neck and I'm coming out with words I didn't think I knew. He says *te quiero* and I don't know whether he means 'I want you' or 'I love you', and then I realise, Jesus, I'm actually going to get him there just by doing this, and that's mental because surely that really only happens in films, and then I'm thinking, shit, so maybe he has done this before.

His eyes are rolling and he's starting to shake and then he twists his torso awkwardly, and now I think I'm doing something wrong, but I look up and he's grabbed the picture on the bedside table, a faded reproduction of a renaissance Madonna-with-child, and as he places it gently face down, I look him straight in the eye, pull his hips into mine, and we both come at the same time, me inside him, him all over my chest.

I look at the clock and see I've been in Gernika for forty minutes.

Jon Russell Herring is a translator and teacher based in northern Spain. He was joint recipient of the 2023 Stephen

Spender Prize, and his English versions of queer Argentine poetry and Brazilian fiction have appeared in magazines and journals. His own experimental autofiction *Quartet* was published in 2024 and he is currently working on a longer piece about gay life in the 90s.

The Old Man and the Sea Serpent – Tejas Yadav

'I've come here to die,' he said, lowering his gruff voice to a raspy baritone. He liked to mess with those children.

'Oh, why do you say that, grandpa?' one of the muddy-nosed boys whimpered.

'Grandpa? I've told you, I'm *not* your grandpa!' he shot back through gritted teeth. 'Your grandpa's already dead.' He protruded his eyeballs, affecting senility.

'No he isn't,' the youngest, a swarthy girl in a pink pinafore skirt, shouted back. 'You're lying, his grandpa is absolutely kickingly noisily alive!'

'Not for long,' the old man retorted. 'Go ask your mothers.'

The band of village children gawked, the little ones afraid of this impending doom he'd now cast upon their patriarchs. Others, often older, were shrewd and restless, asking more adult questions.

'You've come to die. Fine. So you have money to leave us?'

He laughed at the pragmatism of the innocent and needy.

'I have nothing to give you, except stories. But you probably don't want to hear any—'

'We do!' they exclaimed in unison. He held up a stern finger. The noisy audience fell silent.

A murmur rose from the back of the group.

'Were you a famous man, Grandpa?' the same feisty girl burst forth. Little Shanti was his favourite.

'No, ha! Famous folk don't come to die *here*,' he replied, eliciting a mischievous smile from her.

*

The sea languished, a sleepy mirror that concealed a jade-coloured shield against gorgons in the morning sky. Fishing boats bobbed like gulls at the horizon. A cool breeze swept up the sun-burnt leaves on the sand, whirling in eddies along an uninterrupted necklace of coconut trees around the marina. In an hour, the rising torpor of the morning would bake the beach a new patina of white. On this mirage, occasionally, a seagull landed, squawked and flew away. The children would run off to school shortly, leaving him all alone. For now, though, he held court on a cool stone porch that ran along the exterior of his hut, shaded from the glare of the sand. He sprinkled it with water every morning, rising at dawn. Only the heat made him suffer more than his solitude.

*

The village lay along a quiet strip of a famously touristic state, known by all hippies and Instagram influencers in search of themselves in a subcontinental tidal land. Here, visitors, seabirds, waves, memories – all was ebb and tide. The village kids came for a swim at the beach before school, tumbling in the sand every morning. He knew them by their faces first and, slowly, by their characters. They approached him, dancing with their dark faces out of the sea.

Shrill like the mournful black crows, a bell in the village church would ring out at eight in the morning. Mothers would descend upon his porch, baskets of fresh catch on their heads in wicker baskets. The husbands, fathers and uncles, tanned darker than their women and children, could be seen in the distance as they heaved multicolour, hand-painted boats back to dry land. Before the sun became a hammer, all the protesting progeny would be rounded up, coerced back home with sharp vernacular expletives and the occasional whack on the backside, and sent off to the local school. Every morning, except Sunday when school was out. Sundays anguished the old man; nothing stirred and dying didn't feel like a joke after all.

*

During the day, he mostly slept inside the refreshing stone walls of his hut. A local broker had offered it to him, in exchange for some of his life's savings. It was modest but it would do. In a corner of the solitary space sat a plastic, fluorescent-green garden table and matching chair, sleeping untouched in sand and dust. He wiped it down with a wet cloth, removing years of grime. It felt like turning back a clock. An insipid halogen bulb hung in the living-room-bedroom-every-room space, moths madly in love with its hazy yellow glow. As for the army of mosquitoes, he burned sandalwood incense offered by the garrulous lady who sold bright marigolds on the church steps. He bought her flowers twice a week, only to stay and talk to her.

*

Three ugly and mediocre hotels sat squarely on the seafront like the famous monkey trio, attracting a motley crowd: international globetrotters with passport-privilege and, evermore, travellers from other parts of his own country trying to escape to nature.

Escape what?

He found attempting to forget birthed its own heartbreak, a greater sorrow. He simply yearned for nothingness but it never came. The future was biting the tail of the past, encircling him, now. A sea serpent coiling under the swinging lamp in his hut.

* * *

Late at night, when sleep didn't bed with him, he turned on a rusty radio bought in the village market, old movie songs echoing in the moonlight, syncopating with bedtime cries of seagulls outside. Silence unnerved him. Words he'd read in another lifetime haunted him: in a period of despair, there is no greater misery than the memory of bygone joys.

What good does pining bring? So, he told people he was dying, not regretful.

*

'Where are the others today?'

Rain clouds hovered ominously over the ribbon of coconut trees.

'At school, the others have to stay back and study more,' little Shanti proclaimed with a smirk. She'd come with her best friend, a mousy, dour-faced girl, around the same age.

This companion rarely spoke, fixedly observing the old man with doleful, brown eyes.

'Grandpa, this is Uma.'

'Hmm, hello Uma,' he said. Uma simply glared back. 'And your mothers know you two are here, after school?'

Shanti nodded although he suspected the scheming imp; she was a notorious mischief-maker even at that tender age. But he liked her sly, rebellious streak. Ironic, he thought. Maybe some things do change with time.

'Today you have to tell us, Grandpa. Where are your children? Grandchildren? Will they visit?'

Always the same questions. Shanti could be incorrigible.

'All dead.' He pursed his lips in consternation.

Uma, the quiet watcher, scowled. Shanti's expression turned from alarm to complicity; her knowing smile disarmed him.

'Now do you want to keep on with your silly questions or do you care for a story?'

'Story!' Shanti boomed, tugging on the other girl's arm. Uma looked bored. Without waiting for a confirmation, Shanti added, 'She wants, I want!'

They sat with him on the porch ledge, one girl on each side, facing the cobalt afternoon sea. The tide was coming in and a few tourists walked up and down the beach after mid-day. A white woman ambled aimlessly, holding a lover's hand. The pall of monsoon had departed, some straggling clouds lingered like wisps in the ether. The leaden sky threatened rain any moment. Far away, near the horizon, volleys of seagulls rose through acrobatic air funnels.

He cleared his throat. The story was a mask.

Hidden and deceitful.

*

'Once upon a time, an old king lived in his grand palace. It stood on the seaside on a big rock, looking out to the heavens and oceans. He had a daughter—'

'A princess,' Uma interjected meekly.

'So you do speak,' he guffawed. 'Yes, a *princess.* Now don't interrupt me.'

Shanti ogled at her friend and Uma resumed looking at her feet, dangling above the ground.

'The king loved this daughter a lot. More than the sun loves the moon. He never wanted anyone to harm her or take her away. So he commanded his ministers to erect walls around the castle—'

'You said palace,' Uma mumbled under her breath while pulling on her big toe.

'Shhhh,' rebuked Shanti, getting up to change sides, sliding between the two of them.

He scoured the faces of the two girls, wondering if he'd mistakenly discerned the streak of resistance in the wrong child.

'The walls were manned by soldiers, day and night. No one was allowed to visit the princess without the king's approval. She had all the world's toys, animals, birds, luxuries. The king felt relieved and happy but not the princess. In fact, each time he saw her, she seemed to be sadder than the last. Withering away like a rose in the snow.'

He watched a question form on Uma's face but one stern look sideways from Shanti overruled any inquisitions.

He felt Uma growing on him, but he knew it was merely a ghost of the past catching up.

'The princess was lonely. She had no friends. She ached to go outside the walls, see the world outside her golden cage. Her maids and ladies-in-waiting played with her but she needed something else. Her father tried to placate her with all manners of entertainment: music, jugglers, jesters, books, jewels, dancers but she remained decidedly unhappy. Then one day, seeing as she had grown older and was no longer a little girl like you two, the king decided to marry her off. He invited all the princes from neighbouring kingdoms to have an audience with her. Yet the princess didn't even glance at those great noblemen. The king wished her mother, the queen, were alive to help him but she'd died many years ago. He was left with a child he did not understand. Though he loved her, she was a mystery to him and at times her stubborn nature angered him.'

He took in a sharp breath, closed his eyes for a moment, blinked, exhaled deeply before continuing.

'Time passed and soon the princess had become a clever, beautiful and skilled woman. When the princess was nearly the same age as the departed queen on the day of her wedding with the king, something unexpected happened.'

The first few cold drops started to trickle down his face, like tears from the thatched roof of his hut, a carpet of dried coconut leaves. The beach had cleared out, people started running back to their unsightly hotels.

'We better continue tomorrow. It's starting to pour,' he said. Shanti protested, Uma said nothing.

'You girls ought to go home, it might rain for a long time and I don't even have an umbrella.'

Shanti argued that their mothers knew where they were. The old man conceded defeat, secretly glad the duo wanted to wait with him.

Under the awning of his verandah, a wide strip of the porch remained dry. Together, the three watched clouds burst into a heavy downpour. Thunder split the sky. Uma smiled widely, bewitched, still reticent. Shanti clapped furiously, thrilled at the spectacle. The sea was turning angry and daylight seeped away, like night had fallen prematurely. He had to restrain Shanti from jumping outside of the dry verandah. The monsoon had reared its head one last time.

*

'On that fateful day, a golden-haired fisherwoman visited the fortress,' he continued over the noise of rain coming down in sheets.

'She was tall, fair and green-eyed like a snake. No one knew where she came from. A beauty never seen in those lands. All the king's ministers and soldiers were agog with her beauty. But she was not interested in their charms. She was a strong-minded woman, smart and focused only on business. In front of the king, she claimed to have the best, freshest, most delicious and rarest fish of all—'

'Ha, just like my papa,' Uma whispered to Shanti, making her giggle.

'—but she would offer them to the king on a single condition.'

He paused, watching the girls twiddle their fingers expectantly.

'She'd heard of the young princess: her elegance, grace, wisdom and broken heart. This strange fisherwoman demanded to meet the princess. For like her, she too was—' he hesitated, '—friendless, in a world of men. She was looking for someone like her—'

'A sister?' Uma piped up.

He looked at her, searching for the contours of a forgotten face.

'More than sisters.'

The girls looked confused. 'Anyway, did the king agree?' Shanti asked.

'The king saw no problem with this arrangement. Out of love, he would do anything for his daughter's happiness.'

Uma was busy rubbing her knuckles but she cocked an ear when he responded. Had she detected the false note?

He was back with the past; a memory floated, an argument. A breaking point, nebulous and painful. A girl lost to him.

Shanti became agitated at the lull in the story. She poked, jolting him back to the rainy present.

He kneaded his stiff neck, peeling away the coils of a sea serpent tightening around him.

*

'The king soon received news that the princess was seen smiling, after many long years of despair and sorrow. The cure, incredibly, was the company of that enigmatic other woman. So the king ordered the fisherwoman to be elevated to the position of a lady's maid. She would, henceforth, live in the fortress with the princess.'

Thunder cracked a whip and this time both girls shrieked. Uma's gaze unsettled him. He laughed to hide his own heartache.

'The king was finally at peace. The princess was delighted with her new companion and the fisherwoman was joyous in her new life. Over the years, their friendship blossomed and it saved everyone.'

He winced, then lied, 'The End.'

Shanti applauded, laying her tiny head on his arm. Uma was biting her lower lip, a storm brewing inside as outside. She leaned forward to look at him. 'I have a question,' her hesitant voice said.

'Ignore her,' said Shanti. 'I *love* happy endings! Thank you, it was wonderful. And you see, no one died,' she said with a grin.

'The queen had died,' Uma said peevishly to no one. 'Maybe the king died later too, he was old. Old people die.'

She let her words hang there in the silence. Her eyes fixed on the sea changing from grey to violet to bottomless black. He understood the girl's spite, her thirst for the truth she suspected he was withholding.

*

No one spoke as the rain fell in a deluge that could end the world.

Shanti played with her skirt and eventually fell into a deep slumber on the porch ledge. Drops fell in a rhythmic melody. The sky continued emptying itself for an hour. The old man glanced at the two little girls on the porch, an invisible serpent around his neck. Uma glanced askance from her corner, scrutinising his face with those doe-shaped eyes. He feigned a snore and she looked away, towards the horizon.

Three strangers sat in a storm like fish swimming in the silence of a bowl slowly filling up from the sky.

*

He knew the king was dying.

The princess went away to be with the fisherwoman.

*

It was Uma who found him the next morning, crumpled in a heap by the side of his hut.

She ran back to the village, and for once, her small voice was heard shouting a strange phrase:

'The old king is dead! The old king is dead!'

*

All the children came to say goodbye to 'Grandpa'. Shanti, most of all, was inconsolable. Uma kept her head bowed and chewed on the hem of her skirt. The villagers asked the broker; no, the old man had not named any next of kin or contacts. No one knew which gods he believed in, if any. So they buried him in the old cemetery behind the church. The woman who sold flowers laid a wreath of marigolds.

No one came for him.

*

Afterwards, the village mothers went through the affairs in his hut. They stumbled upon something curious in the abandoned notebook on his plastic green table. It was of little interest to the villagers but Uma begged to keep it. The next day she took it to her school headmistress who could read.

On every page he'd written the same word. A girl's name.

On the last page, upside down, in a smudge like he'd scribbled it down in haste, extracting it from a buried memory: a telephone number.

*

'It's for you,' she whispers, pulling back her blonde hair into a tight bun. 'The woman says it's very important and she doesn't have much time.'

Groggy-eyed day has broken over the wintry landscape. Far away, ice caps glisten in the early morning sun. They have planned to go for a hike later that day. People in her mountainous homeland love their hikes and she isn't going to let her girlfriend weasel out of one today.

'Who is it?' Aditi asks, rising from her pillow.

'A broker from Goa, I think? I didn't follow her accent but I think it might be about—', she says, handing over the telephone before planting a kiss on Aditi's forehead.

'I'll go make us some coffee,' she whispers before slipping out of the room in her nightgown.

A static crackle, the telephone catches a far-off intonation, the sound of heavy traffic in the background. When she walks back into the room with two steaming cups, Aditi is sitting motionless at the edge of their unmade bed. The blonde woman watches Aditi tense up, perhaps hearing the unfamiliar voice, as sounds of a country she left behind come whooshing in. Aditi's dark eyes are watching something out of the window, the whole time, not a blink. The silence becomes another blanket of snow after Aditi hangs up.

She's about to break the spell, but finds her own lips trembling. 'Babe, who was it? Is everything OK?'

Aditi shuts her eyes in response. A tear rolls down her beautiful dusky cheek. The coffee sits forgotten, losing heat slowly, bitter and dark like the remorse of brittle, unsaid things. Through the narrow windows of their flat, a weak sun catches two women embracing silently. One of them is keening, wondering how two words can so easily orphan her. Again. Morning stretches a bleak arm over the mournful bedroom, the hiking boots forgotten in the hallway. Time becomes an infinite serpent, swallowing the past and present, strangling everything in its hold.

Aditi, I'm sorry. Love, Pa.

Tejas Yadav is a gay, South Asian polyglot whose writing explores identity, alienation and mental health. His poetry, fiction and essays have been featured in Burnt Roti, Queer South East Asia, Gaysi Family, Stellium Literary, Borderless Journal etc. He has lived in Mumbai, Oxford, London, New York and Paris. He likes good coffee and radical thinking. writejas.wordpress.com

Years from now we will meet again–
Anja*Oliver Schneider

Years from now, we will meet again
in the front seats of your white truck.
The worn cushion will recognize me

like an old friend, faded and soft.
You greet me with a look that doesn't wonder
where I've been. Your cheeks will draw

your lips upwards to reveal the edges
of your k-nines. I won't remember sharpness,
only the way your teeth were so close

to my teenage lips, the hunger of first love
that devoured. The image will not sting
anymore, will not be soured by what came

after. We won't wait for touch; our hands will join
in the middle, pulled back by warm Southern summer
nights and confessions. I thought we had lost it,

this youth. That this *you* only existed in my memory.
But here you are, beautiful as ever,
seventeen and ageless. I will look up at you

in only joy, see a star in your green eyes.
By the time I open my mouth, it will already be gone.
I won't have to say anything. You'll already know.

Anja*Oliver Schneider (they/them) is a queer, non-binary trans educator, poet, scholar, and accessible Yoga teacher from a small town in Germany. Oliver's work explores lesbian/trans intersections, trans masculinities, queer abuse, and disability in connection to the body and nature. Oliver is the self-published author of *Non-Binary: An Introduction* and facilitates workshops on LGBTQ+ topics, writing, and mindfulness.

God Redeems – Claire Deacon

When I think back to my time in the cult, I can't help but think of Sarah. She used to sit a few rows in front of me during the sermons, and I was far more interested in contemplating her than whatever was being said during those dull, righteous talks given by upstanding men of the congregation. It seemed to be the same thing every day; every word was carefully chosen to align with our overarching doctrine, every tie carefully straightened by a subservient wife.

The sermon hall was bland and sterile to my nineteen-year-old eyes. White walls, scent of floor polish, posters bearing scripture. I suppose that was the point, there wasn't meant to be anything there that could tempt any of us. I guess they never counted on Sarah.

Of course she was dressed just as modestly as all the other young women, but nevertheless there was an undeniable sensuality to her long, black hair and a hint of mystery in her eyes. More than once I passed the sermons happily gazing at her. Once or twice she caught me looking and before I could tear my eyes away in embarrassment, she would give me a smile that seemed full of quiet mischief. Or maybe that was just wishful thinking on my part.

For a group so obsessed with sexual purity and who condemned any intimacy but married, heterosexual sex, I detected an undercurrent of perversity in my godly brethren. It would begin when a speaker touched on the subject of Armageddon, a perennial favourite. At first the congregation would close their eyes and smile gently, as David or Saul or John described the war that would be waged before the end times. Then, as the familiar story progressed and the speaker described how every soul would be resurrected and judged, my fellows would lean forwards in their seats, hands clasped together, eyes shining with anticipation. And then the climax. The speaker would assure us that we were the ones to be saved. We, the true believers, would have an everlasting place on a newly perfect earth. Our sacrifices would be rewarded, the day was coming soon. At that, those around me would expel a deep breath before leaving the hall awash with serenity, their faith renewed and the collection box growing fat.

For as long as I could remember, the Elders had viewed me with suspicion. I never quite had it in me to comply with their rules the way everyone else did and I've often wondered in the years since why that was. Perhaps it was due to the fact that unlike so many others I wasn't born into the cult, and I could still remember the years of relative freedom I had before my mum got sucked in and they became the arbiters of our lives. I had distant but happy memories of colourful Christmas and birthday celebrations, of sleepovers with friends and learning dance routines to the latest pop songs. Now all forbidden of course.

Or maybe it ran deeper than that. Maybe it was something in my blood. I wasn't supposed to know much about my mother's past life of sin, as she called it, but I had heard enough whispered conversations amongst the congregation to know that there had been a wildness in her, once. And sometimes I felt like she'd unwittingly passed it right on to me.

Although I knew the Elders didn't like me, they never stated their concerns directly. After all, my mother was very loyal and very wealthy, and I'm sure they didn't want to risk upsetting one of their biggest donors.

She, conversely, didn't mind telling me exactly what she thought of me.

'You need to dress more modestly,' she'd snap, whenever I dared to wear a skirt that sat above my knee or a lipstick a shade too bright, 'do you really think you're going to find a godly husband if you keep showing off your body?'

I did not want to find a godly husband. I did not want to find any husband.

After one such row, my mother drove off to God knows where, leaving me alone in the house. In the mood for a quiet rebellion, I clambered up into the loft, squeezed into a tight, dusty corner and dragged out a large, slightly limp cardboard box. This box contained the only items left from my mother's previous life, and I was not supposed to know of its existence.

A delicious thrill went through me as I began pulling out items. Some of them I'd unearthed before; a gold makeup case, a dreamcatcher, letters from people whose writing I didn't recognise. And books; piles and piles of them. Textbooks, poetry books, romance novels. Things that would not sit comfortably alongside the safe, approved literature on our bookcase downstairs.

The romance books were right at the bottom and I hadn't yet had the chance to have a good look at them since discovering this treasure trove. I selected one at random, my pulse throbbing in my ears. There was a half-naked man on the cover, but he didn't interest me. Instead, my eye was drawn to the adoring woman in his arms, looking up at him from beneath flirtatious lashes. I flicked through the book and stopped abruptly at a sex scene. I hadn't been taught much about sex, just enough to know that it was to be kept strictly within a heterosexual marriage, and even then you should really try not to enjoy it.

The woman in the book was definitely enjoying it. The descriptions of her body and the sensations she was experiencing caused a dark, dangerous feeling to grow inside of me. I thought of Sarah. I thought about what it would be like to touch her hair, her face, her lips . . .

A confusing mixture of guilt and yearning pulsed through me and I snapped back to reality. Aware I'd been in the loft for some time, I quickly put the other items back in the box, snuck the book down to my bedroom and hid it at the back of my wardrobe.

*

When I saw Sarah at the next sermon, I blushed. I was too nervous to gaze at her today as I feared the lustful thoughts I'd had about her would be written all over my face. My fear was only compounded when one of the Elders took us both to one side after the meeting. Had they somehow found me out?

'Leah, you know Sarah?'

I nodded and she smiled at me, making me feel even worse.

'Well, we thought it might be nice for the two of you to spend some time together discussing scripture. We know it can be difficult for young women growing up in today's world. Maybe Sarah can give you some guidance about how to remain a child of God.'

That's when I realised what was really going on. He thought the Elders were giving me a veiled caution about my general lack of godliness and a chance at redemption. What they were actually giving me was a gift.

The first few times that Sarah came round to my house for Bible study, my mother was there to observe, so I played along and discussed teachings on modesty and the place of women in the congregation. I would have done or said just about anything to keep seeing Sarah on a regular basis.

Eventually, Mum decided that she could leave me alone with her. I'd been formulating a plan for this very occasion and wasted no time in putting it into action.

'I wanted to ask your advice,' I said, 'I found a forbidden book, and I'm not sure what to do about it.'

She looked concerned but intrigued. I took her up to my room, brought the old romance book out of the wardrobe and placed it in her hands. She looked as if I'd just handed her a vial of poison.

'Where did you get this?'

'I found it in the loft, with Mum's old stuff.'

'We shouldn't be looking at this, Leah. It's things like this that tempt women away from God's path.'

I couldn't help noticing that despite her words, she was taking a long, hard look at the cover. I screwed up all my courage in order to ask her what I really wanted to know.

'But doesn't it make you feel something? Something exciting?'

She paused. 'Yes. That's exactly why it's forbidden.'

I'm not sure who kissed whom, even now, but I do know

that to my intense surprise and relief, we were both as into it as each other.

That first time we just kissed, until we heard Mum pulling up in the driveway. The time after that we took each other's shirts off and after that I guess we thought we had nothing left to lose so we ended up a wide-eyed bundle of trembling, bare skin, squeezed together under the covers on my single bed.

That was the first time I knew with certainty who I was, and that I had to get out of that place.

For the next few months, things between us continued in the same vein. At first I was ecstatic. Maybe we could make our escape together, I thought. But it gradually became apparent that Sarah didn't share my passion for freedom.

Whenever we were alone together, even when we did nothing but hold hands, she'd eventually get this panicked look in her eyes and insist we kneel side by side to pray for forgiveness. My heart really wasn't in it, but I'd kneel next to her anyway and watch her from under my eyelashes. Her eyes would be squeezed shut, her lips would move in silent, frantic prayer and her hands would be clasped together so tightly that her fingernails left angry little crimson moons in her pale skin.

'If we repent, we'll be OK,' she'd say, 'this isn't the way God made us.'

I thought that was bullshit. I didn't understand why she couldn't just enjoy this small piece of happiness we'd found. Maybe, I realise now, she believed in a way I never had.

I have no way of knowing who it was that reported us to the Elders, but I've often thought that it might even have been Sarah herself.

During my hearing I refused to admit to anything, just

sat glaring at the two old men who were telling me over and over again that homosexuality was an abomination and that they could only help me if I repented. Eventually they grew tired of my silence.

'Leah, you leave us no choice. We believe you have blasphemed against God and led sister Sarah astray. You are no longer welcome in our congregation.'

I should have been devastated; my whole world was about to come crumbling down around me. But my sense of relief was stronger than my fear.

Some part of me hoped Sarah would find a deeply buried reserve of courage, but I knew in my heart that she wouldn't be coming with me. She still believed there was something these people could give her, something worth giving up her freedom for. No, she would confess everything. And she would repent.

I've built a good life for myself out of the nothing I had when I was summarily ejected from their 'paradise' ten years ago. There were hard lessons to learn along the way; it turns out there are plenty of people in the world who would seek to manipulate and control you, and they don't just confine themselves to easily-identifiable cults.

But gradually, I found my way. Every time I made a trustworthy friend, every time I took a baby step towards joining the queer community, it felt like more and more of some intrinsic inner me was being revealed, the way sculptors talk about releasing their statues from blocks of stone.

It made me sad to think that Sarah may never get the chance to experience the same. I pictured her trapped inside her block of stone forever, unchangeable and unreachable.

I saw her on a London street on my way to work a few months ago like a phantom from a past life, handing out religious leaflets with two of the old-timers. I don't think the old ones recognised me; I guess I do look pretty different these days, with my piercings and short, colourful hair. But she knew me. I could see it in her eyes.

I froze in front of her, hoping she would say something. That she was sorry, she was ready to leave now, even just that she remembered me.

Instead, she simply put one of her leaflets into my hands.

'God redeems,' was all that she said.

Claire Deacon has been writing for as long as she can remember and has had nineteen short stories published in various anthologies. She enjoys writing and reading about queer love and is currently writing her first sapphic romance novel. She lives in the Midlands, UK where she helps to run bookish groups for the local queer community.

How to Talk to Unicorns – Greg Williamson

There are three things that you need to know. The first was that Declan McCraigie had a way of making you notice him. And the first thing you always noticed was his fat, red arse.

His arse was the kind of crimson you'd see on an old man's face down at The Commercial Inn. It was a round, spotty thing with clusters of pink splotches all over it; it was like the poor bastard had sat bare-cheeked in a bunch of stingies, or had a bad bout of prickly heat. Still, despite its grotesqueness, he paraded it proudly around the school locker room as if his arse was best in show at Crufts. The ugly thing jiggled like some hypnotic strawberry jelly forcing you to look at it while it moved of its own accord, continuing to ripple long after Declan would stop moving.

The second thing was that Declan, every week without fail, used the first ten minutes after gym class as an opportunity to spraff some new story he'd concocted that week. He'd bark his newest tale through the clouds of Lynx Africa and above the chorus of 'bullshit!' chanted by the other boys. Yet, despite his obvious deception, the gobshite with the red baboon arse somehow commanded everyone's complete attention as he cavorted around the locker room like some alpha pack leader. Or a poor drunkard attempting a stand-up routine at an open mic night.

Today, as the other boys around him got dressed back into their school uniforms, Declan spent his usual allocated time screaming about how just that night prior he'd seen a unicorn in his front garden.

'Naw, really,' he yelled defensively above the boys' hysterics. 'It even spoke tae me.'

If Declan ever found that the locker room had erupted into too much chaos and had begun to drown out his ability to fully tell his story, he simply wound his towel into a tightly bound vine and whipped it against some poor chap's cheeks, making them spring from the floor like a startled cat, silencing the room.

'Yer spraffin' shite,' Kyle said, before quickly receiving a lashing across his exposed bum which swiftly shut him up.

'I'm no joking,' he said, bringing the room back under his command, 'I was taking the bins out for my maw, and there it wis at the end of my garden just looking at me.'

'Liar,' an equally loudmouthed Bryce said.

'Am no,' Declan continued, 'It was this pure white thing, with glowing fur and these mad blue eyes.'

He moved through the changing room with this strange swagger, his drooping, hanging apron of a belly the only thing covering his modesty.

'You're an eejit,' Liam Anders said, before quickly covering his arse to avoid a lashing. 'What did she say then, eh?' Another boy yelled.

'Honestly,' Declan continued, 'She was pure asking me to ride her, dirty bitch!'

The boy began slapping his fist against his arse as he galloped across the room, twirling his towel above his head like a lasso, screaming 'giddy up' as he moved.

Declan's gaze locked on me as I sat at the far end of the room, my bum glued to the wooden slatted bench (I would rather take a chance of splinters on my bare cheeks than one of Declan's whippings). I'd already spent the last hour in a piss-filled swimming pool having a ball hurled at my face by a group of angry pit bulls trying to drown me in the middle of a water polo match, so I was hurriedly getting dressed to make a swift exit.

'You believe me, don't ye?' Declan said, making his way over to me as I tugged my wet trunks off, desperately grasping my towel so that it wouldn't spring open and expose me.

'Yes,' I said quietly, attempting to secure my boxer shorts, wishing the interaction would end as quickly as it had started. 'You've got no reason to lie.'

In actual fact, Declan McCraigie had every reason to lie. Since the first day of high school, Declan had made his way to the top of the playground pyramid by being a professional bullshitter. He had once told our gym class that he'd caught Mrs Flannigan (an old boot of a chemistry teacher) hanging frilly, crotchless thongs on her washing line one afternoon last summer. Despite the uproar from doubters at the time, Declan presented a pair of red, lacey underwear from his school bag the very next week and Mrs Flannigan then spent the next half a year being trolled relentlessly with the nickname 'Mrs Fanny-gin' until she was eventually signed off work for the year. To this day, I still believe Declan most likely raided his own mother's knicker drawer for the 'evidence'.

'Aye, I bet you'd love to see a unicorn in your garden,'

Declan said to me, 'bet you'd bend over and take its horn up your poop shoot, ya fucking woofter.'

The room erupted at that point. I dreamed of exiting the locker room, leaving the stench of prepubescent body odour and Declan's red arse far behind.

'See, wee Jamie believes me,' Declan said to the other boys before grabbing my neck and locking my head under his arm. He rubbed his balled fist against my scalp until the crown of my hair was a tufted mess.

'Go on,' Declan continued, as I stood near naked in the middle of the school changing room, 'Tell the lads that you believe me.'

'I do,' I said, 'I believe him.'

With that, Declan released me with a hard shunt as the other boys did little to stifle their laughter. I hurriedly buttoned my shirt, threw on my trousers and raced out of the locker room, without evening tying my shoelaces.

The truth is, I *did* believe every word that Declan had spoken. Because you see, the third thing that you need to know, is that I'd seen the unicorn myself that very same night.

*

The night she appeared had been a frighteningly windy one. Like that scene at the beginning of *The Wizard of Oz* where the house is spun into the air, and the wicked witch cycles past Dorothy's window in the middle of the whizzing tornado.

The trees in the garden rattled furiously, their branches flailing like one of those ridiculous, inflatable car-garage tube men. Outside, someone's wheelie bin from a few doors up had toppled over and had been dragged along the cul-de-sac, sending a spinning cloud of litter into our front garden.

'Jamie,' Mum said, 'would you mind pulling that bin into the garage so it doesn't bash into someone's car?'

I begrudgingly pulled on my slippers and walked into the front garden, as the wind rushed into the house and slammed the door shut behind me. My baggy jammie bottoms battered against my thigh as I walked across the garden to retrieve the runaway bin. It was winter and the sky was already ink black at 5 p.m. And that is when I saw her; her white glow spilled out from beyond the brick wall to the side of the garage.

'Hello,' she said looking up at me, 'Is my hair a mess?'

I blinked at the creature, her unearthly fur sparkling as she moved. The white light around her was blinding, like a halo. Or the motion sensor flood lights above dad's garage. Her coat was a wonderful mix of pristine white fur, with swirls of light grey markings across the bridge of her muzzle that looked like little perfect storm clouds.

'Well,' she said, tilting her head at me in annoyance, 'Aren't you going to invite me in?'

'What are you?' I asked.

'I'm fucking freezing, that's what I am.'

With that, I pulled open the garage door and outstretched my arm, gesturing for the animal to come inside. Quickly, she trotted round the wall, walked up the driveway and stood in the garage amongst the tins of old paints, power tools and boxes of old Christmas decorations.

I flicked the light switch at the back of the room, and her full form was suddenly illuminated by a single, dangling bulb which hung from the joists. Her face, with its startling blue eyes, had a soft pink blush to it – and out of her forehead, like some perfect, precious shell burst a pearlescent spiral horn.

'Where did you come from?' I asked.

'The bin, of course.'

The unicorn offered no further explanation about how a creature of its size had managed to fit inside of a wheelie bin, let alone how it found itself inside the bin to begin with. I found myself nipping at my skin, assuming that the sun would break through my curtains, a bird would chirp loudly outside my window, and I'd wake up in my bed desperately trying to fall back asleep again to see how the strange dream with the unicorn ended.

But no amount of pinching did anything. The unicorn remained at the bottom of my garage, her cyan-blue eyes fixed on me as she brushed her head against an upright garden rake which hung from the breeze block wall, trying to unknot her matted mane.

'You're beautiful,' I said, finally squeezing some words out of my dry, agape mouth. 'You're sweet,' she said with a wink of her white eyelashes. 'Jamie, is it?'

I looked at my arm, which had turned red from the pinching. A fat droplet of blood had burst through the skin and was now sitting on my forearm as a stark reminder that I would not be waking up from this freakish dream anytime soon.

'You know my name?' I said, rubbing my eyes in disbelief. 'Of course I do – you're exactly who I'm here to see tonight!'

'Me?' I stuttered.

'Aye, you!' she said, flashing a wide toothy grin. 'Well, you and some other lad up the road!'

'Another boy?'

'Aye, must be something in the water round here!' She chortled at herself.

The animal strutted around the garage, before pausing to stare at her reflection in the car window. Her silver glow pulsed slowly, bouncing off the car doors and painting the grey walls of the garage with its sparkly sheen.

'Are you a unicorn?' I asked, after a gust of wind tore through the silence in the garage. 'What do you think?' she said with an eye roll, 'I'm not a talking rabbit!'

'Why are you here?'

'Because, dear boy, we've a lot more in common than you might think.'

The unicorn trotted towards the far end of the garage, narrowly avoiding a box of old tools which nearly collided with her hind. She began sinking her rear down towards the ground, folding her back legs underneath her rump as she cosied into the corner.

'Come,' she said, nodding her head at me, 'sit with me.'

I tucked myself into her outstretched fore legs, and rested my head against her strong, warm neck. With my ear pressed against her, I could quite easily hear the peculiar thump of her heartbeat, which pulsed through her like some unworldly disco track, as if it was a song only she knew.

'Talk to me,' she said, her voice vibrating down her neck, buzzing against my head, 'What's wrong?'

'What do you mean?'

'I only appear when I'm needed,' she said with a warm firmness, 'and I think, tonight, you need me.'

The unicorn rearranged herself, shuffling her body so that her face was now in line with mine.

'You've felt it, haven't you?' Her eyes were so kind as she spoke. 'That there is something inside of you. Something special. Something different . . . rare. Am I right?'

She knew she was right.

Her words hit me like a blast from the storm outside. I had not realised it, but my face had turned blotchy and red. Fat, wet globules were rolling down my cheeks and into her mane as she talked.

'Aw pet,' she said, rubbing the side of her cheek against mine, 'don't let anyone dim your light. If it wasn't for people like you, we'd only see stars at nighttime.'

I tried to speak, but was interrupted by the tuneful buzz of the animal's hoof. A diamante watch, wrapped around her ankle, was flashing and beeping to some gleeful beat, like some vajazzled ankle tag.

'Oh shoot,' she said, hitting a button which silenced the thing, 'I've got another appointment to head to.'

She rose to standing and stared at me intently. 'You'll find them,' she said, 'your tribe. Be patient.'

The animal shook out its mane, clicked its four hooves three times, and vanished in a cloud of dusty pink.

'You sorted that bin yet?' Mum's voice rang out from behind me.

'Almost!' I replied.

I walked to the bottom of the garden and looked for the unicorn's glow somewhere on the street. But the only light was that of the yellow streetlamps bouncing off the pavement. I pulled the neighbour's bin into the garage, making a mental note to return it to its rightful owner in the morning once the storm had passed. I inspected the number which had been painted in white spray paint on the front: 179. Declan's house.

*

The school bell rang, and I found myself racing for the gates faster than usual. My red, blotchy eyes were still stinging from the overly chlorinated pool earlier that day.

As I walked through the playground the unicorn's words from the night before were spiralling in my head. *You'll find them. Your tribe.* Surely she didn't mean that Declan McCraigie, with his loud lies and ridiculous swagger, was the same as me? Yet this boy, who had tormented me for years, suddenly felt weak and vulnerable. Every worry or fear I ever associated with him quickly melted away and I felt an unimaginable power knowing that Declan, beneath his machismo, was just like I was. A unicorn.

You see, there is a certain flair that boys like me have – a distinct way of being that cannot be fully hidden with any amount of bravado or masking. It's in the subtleties; a movement in the hips as we walk, thinking no one is looking, or in the limpness of a wrist when we forget, momentarily, not to clench it in a fist. Those little fleeting seconds in class, when locked in an intense task and we slip, chewing on the end of a pencil, or fiddling it between our fingers like something precious to be caressed.

Declan McCraigie was just like me. I'd seen it today in those little, fleeting moments in the locker room. The way his eyes darted around when the other boys got changed, as they bent over to pull their socks on, hoping to get a peek at their hairless gooches. How his little tadger twitched and grew slightly when the other boys stood topless and sweaty; as if his own body was betraying him, revealing his secret. He was good at hiding it though; shoving it down behind loud insults and the ridiculous stories he shouted. But I knew where to see it now. Where to look.

'Oi, Jamie,' a voice yelled from behind me, 'Wait up!'

I turned to see a red-faced Declan racing towards me. I quickly turned my back to him and carried on walking, hoping that the fat blob would tire out and leave me alone.

'I just want to talk to you,' he said, walking beside me, wheezing as he caught his breath. Strangely, the usual Declan was not the boy standing next to me; the cruel joker had been replaced by a quiet, panting boy. He seemed smaller and less oppressive like this.

'She spoke to you too, didn't she?' I said, unsure.

Declan was silent, his eyes fixed on the black asphalt beneath his feet. It was the longest I had ever been in his company when he wasn't filling the space with his bullish voice. After an uncomfortable pause, he gave me the faintest nod without looking up at me.

'Thought so.' I said, 'She came to see me, too.'

With this, his eyes lifted to meet mine. I almost expected this nice, quiet mask to slip. For the next cutting remark or jibe to slip from his lips. For his pack of buddies to pounce out, pointing and laughing at me. But Declan just looked at me in complete understanding.

'Do you mind if I walk back home with you?' Declan asked after a few more strides in silence, his lips turning upwards into a soft smile. 'Need to get my bin back anyway.'

It was an attractive thought, I said to myself.

Maybe, just maybe, I'd found the first of my tribe. And with that, we walked home.

Greg Williamson is a Scottish, queer writer based in London. His play *The Gays Are Trying to Kill Me* was longlisted for the 2024 David MacLennan Award, and his short story *The Princess of Inchkeith* was longlisted for the SaveAs Writers' Award.

When Dysphoria Visits – After '4.48 Psychosis' – Rufus Benedict

These disjunct fragments *I will not drown in dysphoria –*
of dysphoria *but swim in inky expanses –*

Engendering a wish for no gendered agenda
I will speak of it again – treading my way back between
these fragments
A night in which everything was revealed:
They're not broken zir forming hermself

I need to become who I already am . . . I always was who I am.

I'll be your mirror – reflect what you are, in case you
don't know
yet
I read Kae and Kane over and over
To find between the letters that liminal line
Somewhere between here and there —
I'll keep trying to divine

Here I am
And There is my body
Dancing
Back to our selves
In the beating heart
of passing darkness
Singing with hope, holding our own, on the boundary

Speak of intimacy: unknot unknowns from within me
Your fingers, my words:
Body mind soul entwined fluid undone unbound
You're such a good boy
Every compliment affirms me to myself.
Needle-like nails: temporary tattoos tell *trans*gressive
tales: fucking till
gender becomes immaterial Immaterial I'm material.
any form any shape – we can be anything we want

Walking between joy and pain each day
Whilst just trying to maintain the mundane
Across the Heath – a hinterland harbour – our one-time
arbour
Where smoke lingers over the years since you told me
your name that night

'I gnaw my tongue – with which to her I can never speak of this
I miss a woman who was never born
I kiss a woman across the years – the splash of her smile lingers'

When
he/she/they/xie/it/ *Delete, add, invent*
fae visits *as you wish or dare*

I will rest
But for the time being

Now.

Please open the curtains.

Rufus Benedict writes, poeticises, creates, politicises, dances and quotes – though rarely all at the same time (though they'd like to try, now they think of it!) Their writing is referential and irreverent, queer and quirky, and tries not to take itself too seriously – even if it's serious. They live in North Wales, for the time being, and one day they hope to grow up and have a moustache.

The Predicters – Cait Owen

At fifteen years old, I got my first period. I knew what to expect. Every other girl in my P.E. class already had theirs. They'd all raised their hands when Lydia Williams commanded them to admit it. Of course, some of them could've been lying because so was I when I raised mine. I didn't want everyone to know I was so far behind.

Mum got me a book about what would happen to my body years before I found blood in my underwear. I'd looked through it almost monthly, preparing myself for the day it would finally come, this preparation in place for the week of bleeding.

A few hours after Mum found me breaking into the stash of sanitary products she'd built up, she called me into the living room.

Both settled on the sofa, me still getting used to the new feeling of the pad stuck in my underwear, she told me now I was becoming a woman there'd be other things I'd need to prepare for.

'Just keep a few pads in your bag at all times for the next one,' she said.

Of course, I knew this from what I'd eavesdropped from the girls at school.

There was anxiety in her eyes above her reassuring smile as I waited for her next piece of advice.

'I've had to notify our GP you've started menstruating,' she said.

I just nodded, sensing there was more she wanted to say.

She continued. 'Tomorrow, you have a doctor's appointment.'

'With Dr Hussain?' I asked, assuming it would be with the woman I'd been going to since my first vaccinations.

Mum hesitated before taking a breath. 'No, sweetheart. Not this time. Your appointment will be with some new doctors.'

'Why?'

She took a breath. 'Doctor Hussain isn't qualified in the same field as these doctors.'

'Have you had appointments with them before?'

'I have. Probably not with the exact same doctors. But for the same purpose. A long time ago. When I was your age.'

I was beginning to feel on edge.

'They need to do a scan for government records. It'll be useful for you. You'll find out what path your life will take.'

'What?'

She rolled her eyes with affection. 'The rest of your life,' she clarified and reached for my hand. 'This appointment will show you where you'll end up.'

I scrunched my brow in confusion.

'It'll make sense at the appointment,' she said quickly and took a sip of her tea.

I tried to ask more questions. To get her to explain. But she told me all I could do now was wait.

*

The next day at school, I was sat on the stairs by the library with my best friend Aisha and I couldn't hold it in anymore.

While she laughed about the jokes the boys in our class had made during our last lesson before lunch, I couldn't join in.

'What's up?' she asked.

I told her about the strange conversation I'd had with Mum.

'She told me it's something to do with finding out my path.'

Aisha looked down at the stairs before us as I explained, but when I finished she looked at me with sudden unease.

'You know something about this, don't you?' I asked.

She'd begun to twist two strands of her dark hair; a tell-tale sign for her nerves.

She nodded.

'Please tell me!' I pleaded. 'Mum won't say anything. I've got it right after school.'

Aisha looked around to check if anyone was listening to our conversation but, as usual, we were the only ones in this part of the school. Since it was a sunny day, most students wouldn't be caught dead indoors during break.

'Do you remember when I got my first period last year?' she asked.

I nodded.

'Well, Mum told me not to tell anyone but the day after it happened, she told me the same thing.'

'You went to the appointment?!' I asked, louder than I meant to.

'Shhh,' Aisha scolded and her voice dropped to a whisper. 'We're not meant to talk about this!'

'Alright,' I whispered back.

Aisha continued. 'I went to the appointment and,' she paused, 'I saw my future.'

'Your future?'

'Mhm. They do a scan of your body and when it's done, they show you an image of you and who your family will be in thirty years.'

'You saw yourself at forty-five?'

She nodded. 'Well, forty-four,' she corrected, her victory of starting her period before me still alive and well. 'I saw who I married and my kids.'

'Tell me, then,' I urged. 'What's your future like?'

'That's the thing. I can't tell you. If I tell you, it won't come true.'

'That's bullshit,' I laughed but Aisha was serious.

'You'll understand after the appointment,' she said. 'The Predicters will explain everything to you.'

'The Predicters?'

Aisha looked at me pointedly and mimed zipping up her lips.

I couldn't believe she'd kept this from me for almost a year. Did that mean the girls I saw every day in class were all keeping it a secret too?

My thoughts began to spiral on my way to my last lesson of the day. Whenever we spoke about our futures, Aisha and I agreed we would have a boy and a girl of similar ages so they could be best friends too. Now, I'd find out if this would really happen. I'd see the face of who I'd marry. Maybe it'd be one of the boys sitting in the same classroom as me now. That would be a proper love story, right? High school sweethearts. That seemed to be the best trope in the books I read before falling asleep each night. Much better than the doomed loves of tragedies in the plays we read in class. No, I'd find love and have a family. That's what everyone said will make a happy life. Someone to grow old with and kids to take care of you when you're old.

*

Mum and I only had to sit in the waiting room for a few minutes before I saw my name appear on the screen above the reception desk.

Instead of walking down the hall to the same GP office with Mum at my side, I walked past the familiar offices alone and towards a door labelled with the words *Scans in Progress*.

Knocking on the door, I felt apprehensive. I didn't know what to expect.

A woman in a white lab coat opened the door. She was just under five feet tall. I had to look down to meet her eyes when she welcomed me in. It was a strain from my above average height and I found my eyes resting instead on the perfectly straight middle parting of her hair.

'Isla Rothchild. I'm glad you found the right room,' she said in a voice I could only describe as shrill.

I walked in and immediately met with a second lab coat. She was more formidable than the first, a head taller than me and clutching a clipboard. She had an excessively neat appearance with her white coat fully buttoned and her hair tight in a bun at the nape of her neck. Eye contact couldn't be avoided with her sharp gaze taking in my appearance but no words came from the stern line where her lips should have been.

I was still wearing my uniform, usually bearable surrounded by the same colours in the school corridors, but under her gaze, I wished I'd changed into something more comfortable. I wish I'd at least taken off my tie before leaving Mum in the waiting room. I felt like it was growing tighter around my neck with every step I took.

A third lab coat sat on the swivel chair at the desk. She was the median between the two extremes in the appearance of her two colleagues but somehow, her presence triggered the most anxiety in me.

Her fingers hovered menacingly above the computer keyboard where my medical records were held. The prescriptions for courses of antibiotics for repeated tonsillitis, pain killers for a broken arm, and multiple failed attempts at a cure for acne. If the Predicters were going to find out my future they must also have an interest in my past.

'Thank you for arriving on time. We work for the UK Census. We need to ask you a few questions before the scan,' she said.

'Please sit.' The first lab coat gestured to the chair opposite and I quickly took it, welcoming the respite from my shaking legs. It was cold in the room. I should have worn tights under my skirt.

'Your first bleed began yesterday. Is that correct?' the lab coat in the chair asked.

'Bleed?' I asked.

'Your period, dear,' the shortest lab coat clarified.

I felt my cheeks heat up and nodded quickly.

'Are you currently in a relationship?'

'No,' I replied, feeling embarrassed, but not as much as when I'd been asked that at the last sleepover I went to with more girls than just me and Aisha.

The lab coat nodded and typed some words into the computer. I couldn't see the screen but I guessed it was similar to a GP's notes screen when they prescribed you medication. But this time, I'd be prescribed an image of what my future would be.

I held my breath and only allowed an exhale when the next question was asked.

'Sexuality?'

'Straight,' I said quickly. If I was honest, I wasn't sure but this seemed like the safest answer in that office with the three women staring at me. It was definitely the safest answer at school. I could still remember the bitchy remarks when Jenna and Laura were spotted holding hands after school. I'd wanted to defend them but couldn't find the words when all the other girl's comments were so venomous.

A small, satisfied smile appeared on the third lab coat's lips.

'Those are all the questions before the scan,' she announced, aggressively tapping the space bar before standing. 'Please follow me.'

I followed her as she walked to the other side of the office to a door in the middle of the wall, which she opened to reveal another room.

This room was very different from the familiar GP's office; it was clean and bright with plain white walls. In the centre, there was a large white spherical machine with what appeared to be a technologically advanced stretcher sticking out the end.

All three lab coats walked into the room and herded me towards it.

'Please lie down in the centre. The scan should only take a few minutes,' the first lab coat advised.

I nodded and lay back on the pseudo-stretcher, thinking about how Aisha had done this a year before and never told me anything about it. How had she kept this secret for so long? But, then again, she'd told me she couldn't say anything without risking losing the future she saw. What would my future be? I felt a rush of anxiety as the lab coats moved around me, moving my arms and bare legs until I was in the exact centre.

'OK. We're ready,' the middle lab coat said, the first words she'd spoken in my presence. Her voice was raspy, as if she was recovering from a bad cold. 'Stay completely still,' she instructed, finally revealing her thin lips.

She leant over me to press a big red glowing button at the side of the machine. There was a loud beep and the stretcher began to slide in. Soon, all I could see was the smooth white interior walls.

I tried to relax but this seemed to oppose the instruction of staying still. I didn't want to ruin the scan. My future was depending on it. So, I just lay there, rigid, with my eyes glazing over.

Mum was just about to turn forty-five. Had she seen me a few months from now when she'd had this scan as a teenager? Had she seen Dad? Probably not. He was with Mia and their new baby now. Maybe he was in the background? I thought about the anxiety in her eyes when she'd told me about the scan last night. It would probably be insensitive to ask her about it.

'All done,' said the first lab coat as I felt the stretcher moving out of the machine, allowing me to move once again.

I sat up and was confronted by all three women glaring at me.

'Did I move?' I asked.

'Moving is *not* the issue,' the second lab coat sneered. 'It's what we've seen.'

I drew my knees to my chest as if they would protect me from these three women and what they now knew.

'Follow me,' the third instructed. 'We might as well show her. Maybe she can change her path,' she said to her colleagues.

I followed them back to the office. 'What have you seen?'

They didn't answer.

I sat down on the same chair as before and they placed a machine over my head. It covered my eyes so I could only see a blank screen. I felt my body tense, as it had before. Then, on the screen, something appeared. There was someone in the centre of a clean white room, much like the inside of the machine. They were still, as if stuck in a photograph, wearing a thick black jumper and blue dad jeans. They looked a bit like Mum. They had her copper brown hair but it was shorter, much shorter, in a style I could never imagine Mum choosing for herself. They had her laughing eyes but they were Dad's blue instead of hazel.

As I looked harder, I saw something I knew more intimately. A birthmark on the inside of one of their forearms. Brown and about the size of my palm. I wanted to look down at my own arm but, of course, my eyes were blocked from my present. I was trapped viewing my future.

'Can you see why we're concerned?' the voice of the third lab coat interrupted this thought.

'What am I meant to be seeing?' I asked with a shake to my voice.

'Yourself and the family you shall have.'

There was only me. Or at least someone who looked enough like me. But why was I alone? I looked happy. But how could I be happy if I had no family? I expected to see children and a partner but there was only empty space where they should be.

'I only see—'

'Yes,' the first lab coat urged.

I took a breath and admitted it. 'Me.'

I felt the machine being tugged off my head and was again met by the glares of the Predicters.

'You do understand you are expected to procreate,' the second lab coat said.

'To have children,' the first clarified.

I nodded. 'Yes,' I stuttered.

'So why are there none there?' the second urged.

'Maybe I can't have them,' I stuttered. 'We learnt about it in biology. Fertility issues are on the rise—'

The third lab coat cut me off. 'But why do you think there isn't anyone else with you? A partner.'

'I—,' I started but didn't want to admit it.

I thought about the possibility of love a lot. The couples in romantic comedies and the couples still together in my own life. But that was fiction. The truth was I'd never believed in having that for myself. It was uncomfortable, even frightening for someone to have such authority in my life. Maybe I was just a late bloomer. That's what Aisha said. She'd had more than a handful of crushes in the past year alone and a kiss behind the bike sheds with Tommy Baxter last year.

The idea of a romantic relationship, especially a committed one, made me want to scratch at my skin when my nails were at their longest. I'd never experienced the crushes other girls my age gushed about. I couldn't even imagine it. Aisha was obsessed with Josh Delaney and while I could see how she'd be pulled in by his jokes, I couldn't understand why, at her last birthday, she'd wished for him to ask her out when she'd blown out her candles.

'We've had an influx of these cases,' the third lab coat said. 'Girls your age, and some even younger, who see more options now they don't need marriage to succeed. Our job is to ensure you know the statistics. If you follow the rules in this society, you will see a certain number of boxes that need ticking. One, find a mate. Two, procreate. Three, die with your job done to ensure the continuation of the human population. Do you understand?'

But what if I can't love the way everyone wants me to? What if I can't love at all? I knew I couldn't ask it aloud. I couldn't even admit it to Aisha.

'I think so,' I muttered to fill the silence.

'As long as you understand these rules, you may go,' the second lab coat said, in the same rasp.

I stood and walked towards the door with the short lab coat following to open it.

'Just do what's right and you'll have a good life,' she said, her voice so sweet it was sickly.

I stopped and looked back when her hand pushed down on the handle.

'Can I tell anyone about this? What I saw after the scan?' I asked, careful not to reveal that Aisha had already told me.

The three women looked at each other and then the third, back in her office chair, turned to me with a cold smile. 'Of course. Tell anyone you like.'

Cait Owen (they/she) is a writer from East London. They have just completed an MA in Creative Writing at The University of Manchester where their work was published in the fourteenth volume of *The Manchester Anthology*.

Red Devil – Marcella Marx

'This one has to be pushed,' Ana Marie says, looking at me because your eyes are covered by a cold mask. Cold will save your brows and lashes, for now. In any case, you've tattooed them in place and stocked up on store-bought lashes. Disguising *it* is important. 'No one must know,' your mum repeats to you. And no matter how cruel that is, you enact it.

Ana Marie's hands are holding a thick syringe the size of four maxi tampons full of the Red Devil – or Doxorubicin, a clear, bright-red fluid, the same colour as Groselha, the gooseberry squash I used to drink as a child.

'Can we begin?' Ana Marie asks, still looking at me.

'Can we?' I ask, gently pressing your soft hand so you can feel my presence. The softness of your hands was the first thing I noticed about you when we met four years ago. You nod, consenting. I take a deep breath holding the urge to untie you from this tube and carry you away. I inhale as if my lungs could expand to hold everything and I give Ana Marie the go-ahead.

On our way to the hospital, I read a poem on display on the tube: '. . . You were the red cardinal's flight to me, the lentil soup smell, the wildfire radiating and replenishing, replenishing . . .'. At Mile End station, we switched lines, from the green District to the red Central where fresh air is so scarce filling up my lungs took a few stops. We surfaced on a windy London afternoon. The ominous St. Paul's Cathedral dome accentuated my feeling of smallness, juxtaposing it with my need to appear strong. On the windows of Farringdon's high street shops, red teddy bears hugged other red teddy bears with red bows tied to their necks, red balloons, and heart-shaped mugs filled with chocolate roses. Infinite I-love-you and be-my-valentine cards, red hearts and cupids stamped on all advertisement banners. We followed them as if tracing red-drenched breadcrumbs that took us to this alcohol-scented room full of machines, gurneys and nurses dressed in blue.

'Is she okay?' Ana Marie asks as if you were not there. The plastic tube connected to your vein is pumping the Red Devil galore. I repeat the question to you.

'Are you? okay?'

'It burns a little,' you mouth, moving your head towards me, but I can't tell if you're in pain. The cold fitted cap buckled under your chin is tied so tightly that it looks as though you're smiling. Under it, your head is at −31°C.

'I'll go slower,' and, lowering her voice, Ana Marie adds, 'maybe next time the nurse won't be so patient.' And I take it as a sign you and I must toughen up.

Four years ago, we were lying down on the grass under a white blooming, weeping tree reading bits from our favourite books out loud to each other. 'I find you in everything. I whispered the first line of a poem in your ear: 'To read you, I need to escape you . . .' I kept reading till you sealed my lips with your mouth. Poems have always made sense of us.

'Could you bring me some hot tea, please . . . to prevent me tasting the Red Devil,' you murmur, raising your hand to show me where you imagine the door is, but instead pointing to a man lying on a gurney opposite you – the only other patient who's brought a companion – a woman who has displayed baby carrots, hummus, olives and an assortment of bite-sized fruits on his table. No Skittles, hazelnut wafers, or Ritz crackers. I run outside to fetch your hot tea while making a mental note for a healthier snack next time.

While you sip your hot tea, another patient sips through a can of Coke. Comfortably reclined on her gurney and oblivious to the tube attached to her arm. She flips a magazine as if she were at the hairdressers. The left arm seems to be everybody's preference. The man beside you and all the other seven patients are plugged left. They slouch, settling down to their routines, calling the nurses by their names. 'Yes, love,' the nurses reply, pushing wheeled carts with gauze, alcohol solution and fluid bags. Unlike them, you swivel left and right, up and down in your gurney as if lying on a nest of ants. The beeping of the machines startles you, not them. Half asleep with his headphones on, the patient on your left could be sunbathing in Jamaica. You too will need to adapt.

'Are you sisters?' Ana Marie asks, halfway through the syringe. I shake my head, thinking: not again. The other day at the hospital, an older woman started by asking this same question, but after running out of options, she asked, 'Mother and daughter?' We laughed at home afterwards remembering her bewilderment after you explained, 'Girlfriends'.

'Girlfriend,' you repeat through your clenched teeth to Ana Marie today, adding, 'It's a narcissistic disorder.' Ana

Marie smiles. I don't. This is an old joke. You use it to assuage the awkwardness of people assuming two dark-haired women at the hospital together could only be sisters.

The first time you told me you were sick, I sobbed, imagining your soft hands and your breasts disappearing and, together with them, that version of me, the person I was with you, would also cease to exist. The first time *you* cried was when you failed to locate a support group. 'I don't belong anywhere,' you told me, reading through the options, 'The black women's group, the Muslim women's group, the mature women's group.' Your need to exist was like a call from the wild.

'Create your own group,' I said, 'The young-beautiful-dark-curly-haired-lesbian-women's group.' Your smile was short-lived, but I took it. As I took you calling me '*Mamma*' the other day, scared that the incision under your arm, where they cleared your axilla of all your lymph nodes, was oozing a red-brownish liquid. I dashed out of the room and brought you a pad that I taped under your arm. 'A pad? Such a good idea!' And then you thanked me with a non-mamma kiss. I know you'd rather have her here, but that would mean having to reveal *it* to your family, as if *it* were some sort of embarrassment.

What would Ana Marie, the older woman at the hospital, think about me filling up all roles, all the missing parts, improvising a mother's cloak to protect you? I don't mind shapeshifting for you, but I miss being *the one* I was four years ago under that white weeping tree.

'My left hand is numb,' you say, taking your right hand towards the left in an attempt to wake it up. Ana Marie stops you just before you uproot your vein. Momentarily, the tube attached to your arm is empty.

'It's her body fighting the Red Devil. That's why we have to push this one,' Ana Marie says, her hands quickly back pumping the Red Devil in. I place my wool cardigan under your left hand. 'Is this better?' I ask. 'I'm freezing,' you say. I cover you with a blanket and my coat, but your hands are still cold. 'You'll get used to it,' Ana Marie says.

One by one, the machines' beeps are setting off. The nurses go from gurney to gurney unplugging the veins and arms from needles and tubes, dabbing and pressing against skin to contain blood. Then they discard the patients' stained cotton pads into a clinical waste bin where all their blood will mix. The old man in front of you bursts into laughter when the nurse hands him the anti-nausea medication, Domperidone, the anti nausea medication. 'DON Peridone,' he repeats. The woman reading the magazine fake gags when the nurse offers her the anti-nausea drugs. 'Poison,' she says in her broken English and refuses to take them home. One by one, your fellow patients stand up, put on their coats, grab their bags and walk out. Your machine is the last to beep. I remove your eye mask and cold cap but red lines remain engraved on your forehead and around your nose. 'I'm nauseous,' you tell Ana Marie. 'Rest a little,' she says, 'and it will go away, we've already given you anti-nausea meds.'

'I feel I have to throw up,' you tell me, pointing to the armchair where I've been sitting for the past four hours. The creamy leather seat is smudged red. 'Was that you?' You ask.

'Yes . . .' I say, hiding the stain with my jacket. 'I completely forgot to change my pad.'

'There's nothing to be ashamed of, it's just blood,' you comfort me as I scrub the seat with an alcohol-soaked gauze. Stupid tears brim over my eyes. My period won't sync to yours anymore.

You start throwing up the hospital bathroom while Ana Marie has dinner in the side room. Your body wants the Red Devil out. Ana Marie needs fuel in to care for the next batch of patients. 'Remember to flush twice or enough times till it's not red anymore,' Ana Marie blurts, shielding her pie-stuffed mouth with her hand.

You hold my arm and we walk to the elevator. 'Welcome to the cancer express,' a man says while we board the lift on the seventh floor. 'The happiest time of the day is when we take it to go back home,' he continues. I nod, feeling the weight of the C word taking up all the available space. You hold on tight to my hand as if preparing for departure.

'I'm sorry I won't be able to kiss you on Valentine's Day.' You whisper in my ear as we get on the bus. 'Ana Marie says I'm poisonous,' you tell me, your head resting on my shoulder. I tilt my face right, offering you my cheek. With your head resting on my shoulder, I reach for my phone. 'She spreads her arms allowing the wind to carry her. Looking down, she wishes she had never left the ground. Looking up, she wishes she could fly higher.'

'Take down the love letters from the bookshelf, the photographs, the desperate notes, peel your own image from the mirror. Sit. Feast on your life.' 'Love After Love', I read to you as the red double-decker bus number 8 takes us back East.

Marcella Marx, a fellow of the London Library Emerging Writers Programme, holds an MFA from Birkbeck. Her fiction has been recognized by the 4thWrite Prize, the

Tennessee Williams & New Orleans Literary Prize, the Berlin Writing Prize, and the New Voices Award. Her short stories have appeared in The Georgia Review and The New Voices Anthology. She is currently working on her second novel.

The Last Hurrah – Araba Aduah

I stand before you, a newly out lesbian
        mourning, with shame

an infinite access to cis-het men
or rather
the privilege that accompanies them
like a little pet

I dress myself up for my date tonight.
Which earrings will he prefer . . .
        Should I
tape my nipples down so as not to distract him, or disgust him?

This self-consciousness is fun today(?) for the first time.
Last day of school vibes.

He messages me:
'The UberX is on its way, I'll wait for you outside the restaurant. See you soon.'

The absence of anticipation
good for the nervous system, bad for my will to live.

The car arrives.
This soft life oh! It is one I will miss.

Note to self:
book driving lessons asap.

He opens the car door and I'm welcomed by a cheeky face
Self-assured and optimistic about what the next few hours
will look like
and feel like, for both of us.

He tries so hard to make me feel special
If only he knew just how special he is.

He is the chosen one,
the final act,
My coup de grâce.

No more hiding my period paraphernalia
No more being sure I'm the better
person in the relationship
No more having to secretly pre-lube my vagina
No more manic-pixie-dream-girling
my way into a free trip to Crete
No more absent anticipation
No more forced eye contact while cheersing because
if you don't it's seven years bad whateverthefuck
No more living vicariously through
him while he fucks me

No more fake laughing and fake everything
No more getting away with flirting with our waitress

Araba Aduah (she/they) is a multi-disciplinary artist and writer from South London. Her work often comes in the form of poetry, short story, screenplays, video and music production. You'll most likely find her running for the bus or watching Married at First Sight.

Under the Table – Aimz Rushton

I am hiding under a spare table at the back of the classroom. Under more optimal conditions, this would likely be a good spot to hide. Unfortunately, the history hut is flanked by huge windows running left to right. The floor is also elevated above ground level, meaning that it's actually easier to spot someone, say, crouching on the carpet than sitting normally at a table.

That's the problem with gut instincts: there's no time for logical thought.

'Oi! She's over there!' BANG BANG. The noise startles a tall blond boy with acne scars across his cheeks. He's annoyed but his eyes follow where Stacey is pointing. Towards me, crouching under the table. Horrified, I avert my gaze to the grey carpet, starting to pat like I'm searching for something. Stacey either doesn't notice or is undeterred: 'She wants to ask you something!' He frowns at her through the thick plexiglass. Despite Stacey indisputably possessing the biggest gob in our large, noisy year group, he struggles to hear her.

Thankfully, Mrs Clough returns to the room: 'Stacey, stop that banging!' She takes in the scene: three girls standing at the far window, looking out, acting giddy. Me crouched under the table. Everyone else sitting where they were before she left the room. She sighs. Fortunately, this is far below the usual level of disruption she faces: 'You three, sit back down. Amy, get up from under there.' The embarrassment I feel is massively outweighed by relief. I don't have to be forced into asking out this boy I am pretending to fancy. Another opportunity will likely present itself; for now, I'm off the hook.

It was so much easier in prepubescent years: then, when asked who I fancied from a particular boyband, I'd either make the excuse that they looked too much like my cousins (East 17) or just pick the one no one fancied (Gary Barlow). In classic baby dyke tradition, all my popstar and actor crushes were non-threatening, floppy-haired boys in their 20s with soft features. And a penchant for flannel shirts.

In my first years of high school, fancying boys was just a lark, a boredom buster. Me and Leanne would flick bits of paper at the heads of our male friends to make them look, while we feigned innocence before snorting with laughter once they turned back. Or ask inane or surreal questions to start a dialogue. When the hand-me-down GCSE Literature textbooks were distributed, mine and Leanne's desk was magically bestowed with a copy previously owned by a sixth form boy we stalked around the football field. The snatching back and forth and claims of homework custody went on until he finished his A-Levels and left.

Now I'm fourteen and this has all gone terribly wrong. I wasn't prepared to hit the stage where 'fancying someone' progressed to 'and then doing something about it'. Now people are actually coupling up for weeks, months even. They are boyfriends and girlfriends in the way that doesn't just involve holding hands on the school bus and then breaking up on the dance floor of the school disco. This is kissing with tongues, people sticking their nose in your business, public displays of physical intimacy. This is hell.

By this time, I am getting crushes on girls. These crushes aren't frequent but cannot be admitted and certainly not treated as a lark. After two years, our year group is rearranged, meaning that I escape my regular tormentors and make new friends. Amongst these new groups, there is one girl I'm particularly invested in becoming friends with. Like me, she styles herself after the music she loves, although her preference is for metal and classic rock. Soon I find out that we're actually related (second cousins or similar); I put my attraction down to some kind of primal recognition. Case closed: not gay, just genetically sensitive. This won't be the last time that sapphic inclinations are discarded to the back of my mind.

In my mid-20s, I have free access to several therapy sessions with a trainee counsellor via one of my employers. After *so very nearly* coming out to myself a year before, I tentatively offer the possibility that maybe I am asexual, maybe even just not attracted to men. The trainee immediately shot back: 'No, that's an excuse for your fear of intimacy.' Oh. So *not* asexual or gay then. I am disheartened.

In my late twenties, I am partaking in cognitive behaviour therapy courtesy of the NHS: I am assigned to a very young therapist. During the background questions in our preliminary session, her eyebrows raise during my rushed account of my sexual experiences to date. I already feel ripped open at having to divulge this part of my life: the silence that follows the eyebrow raise leaves me wretched. However, today she is talking about exposure therapy: what is something that gives me anxiety? I mention how much I hate dating, how I find the actual date part tedious, how expected intimacy makes me physically recoil. How the guilt I feel when I finally say 'thanks but no thanks' is soon swamped by relief. I am practically willing her to ask if I'm perhaps seeking the wrong audience. Instead, she drops the dating phobia and we agree on singing lessons.

Understandably, I felt angry about this assessment – or lack thereof – for years. If only those young therapists had fully explored what I'd said and didn't say, given it some consideration. Then I remember that we were part of the same generation that came of age with Section 28 still in place. We grew up in an environment where being gay or queer or trans couldn't be discussed seriously at school without fear of somehow 'promoting' a deviant lifestyle. I wasn't even aware of Section 28 until after I left school; I didn't join the dots as to how it impacted me until much later.

It is two decades since I hid under the table during History: I'm watching the first season of Drag Race UK. The queens are partaking in the routine heart-to-heart which sometimes has an LGBTQ+ history slant to Educate the Children. Divina De Campo has been prompted to talk about their experience in school, as a child and latterly as a teacher. Divina's experience chimes with mine, such as being a target for liquid, food, phlegm and unimaginative name-calling. I'm not even thirty-five and this is making me feel ancient. Then Divina contextualises this abuse to their fellow contestants: 'Because of Section 28, a lot of teachers felt they couldn't step in. It did a lot of damage to people like me.' My stomach drops; a bomb goes off in my brain. Then the tears come.

As a teenager, I could never understand why teachers

would never intervene when they saw me being bullied: most often, the bullying would happen in classrooms. During the worst lessons, I would sit nearer to the teacher's desk, in the vain hope they might interrupt whatever was happening. I was very bitter about their lack of action for years; it never occurred to me that some teachers had no idea how to navigate homophobic bullying under Section 28. I thought back to the teachers who did support me: they were all experienced with tried and tested ways of discreetly handling problems. Arguably, the bullies were acting 'correctly' by punishing us for being different. Not that it worked.

I wouldn't be erased: I walked through those corridors every day with my head held high (quite an achievement with all the leather collars, metal beads and dog-tags around my neck). Never blending into the background, my hair was short, dyed flame red. My make-up was immaculately applied, albeit the opposite of 'natural': bright greens, royal purples, even pinks and oranges. My hands became weapons: long, strong nails ready to gouge and bulky rings on each finger and both thumbs. The regulation shirt was abandoned for band T-shirts hidden under the authorised sweatshirt, keeping what I loved close to my chest. I was hated, I often hated myself, but I refused to disappear. Eventually, I'd stop hiding from myself too.

At fifteen, I'm savvy enough to spot a more eligible target: a boy in the upper sixth form with bright blue hair, dark clothes and an arty sensibility. More importantly, he seems affable and someone I could be friends with. It will turn out that both of us are gay, although he'll realise that sooner than I. But that is a few years in the future. When I look back, I remember excitedly speaking on the phone, happily arranging a not-quite-date. It strikes me now that I didn't feel any of the revulsion or anxiety that I'd later associate with attempting to date men. We never did kiss and we didn't 'go out' but we held each other upstairs at the local indie club, the location of our not-quite-date. We didn't need to hide from one another.

Aimz Rushton (they/them) is a recovering academic and ongoing pop culture obsessive. After publishing scholarship on contemporary African fiction and mental illness in literature and music, Aimz is currently writing a comedy memoir about grief, trauma, and obsessive fandom. Aimz's writing can be found at their Disco & Dissociation newsletter (https://substack.com/@aimzrushton).

Dining Table (Sold as Seen) – Tom Marshman

For the last month, I've lived with two sets of tables and chairs in my tiny flat. Like a restaurant without any diners. I sit alone at one of the tables. One that I have known since I was a child, where I wouldn't be allowed to leave until I had finished my greens. Where just before, in my teenage bedroom, my mum had asked me in a hushed tone, 'Are you gay?'.

We talked it through, eventually deciding together not to tell Dad, knowing he wouldn't be ready to hear it. Afterwards, as if to soften the moment, she asked me what I wanted for dinner, then cooked a frozen pizza with oven chips, my favourite, and served it on that familiar table and we ate in silence.

The table is a bit of a knock-off, a repro antique with opulent curves but look on the underside and you'll see the exposed chipboard. I run my fingers over the tabletop with its fake marquetry, worn down from constant use. I try to remember when it stopped being the family table and I inherited it, sometime in the late noughties.

I think of everything that has happened around that table. I think about how my dad used to regularly shout down, 'Do you want some carrots up your end?' and how that joke came to an abrupt end when he found out he had a gay son. But I'm no longer in the mood for the Victoriana style – the dark wood, the red velvet upholstery. I prefer something more 70s, like wicker, chrome and a lighter tone of wood, just like my new set.

A notification goes off. It's about the listing of the dining table and chairs I put on a marketplace site. I've been trying to give them away for free for over a month, but no takers.

The message is from Jeevanee.

'Is it still available?'

'Yes.'

'I am interested, can you send me the address please?'

I try to text 'I am in Old Market,' but when I type 'Old Market' the predictive text changes it to 'Old Wounds'.

I correct.

She replies, 'I don't know lots of areas because we came here from India. I live in BS13.'

BS13 is an area on the edges of the city; it has a bad reputation. I have heard reports of knife crime. It's an area that the newcomers into the city avoid.

Jeevanee tells me she wants to collect the table and chairs ASAP.

'Do you have a big car?'

'A Honda Jazz.'

This doesn't mean anything to me.

Regardless, we agree she'll come today and hope it fits in the Honda Jazz.

Two hours later: 'Can I park here?'

I step out onto the street, in my silk dressing gown thrown over my tracksuit trouser, an outfit put together not for practicality but for gazing out of the window feeling philosophical or flicking through one of my many books that sit in piles around my flat. I see a woman who I guess must be Jeevanee standing by a car, in a puffer coat and jeans. She looks kind, and exhausted. Her hair is scraped back into a ponytail; she is with a man who I presume is her husband, moving things around in the boot of the Honda Jazz. In the back seat, there's a boy, who I think must be about fourteen years old.

She shakes my hand and introduces me to her husband.

He's tall, with a half-grown beard and hunched posture. He smiles and shows a big gap in his teeth. They both look at least ten years younger than me but seem full of responsibility and the weight of big life decisions; they make me feel bourgeois. They're dressed practically, to get things done. I wonder about what brought them to Bristol. I invite them into my flat, along with their teenage boy who is so shy he doesn't look at me. His awkwardness fascinates me. There is a fragile beauty in some teenagers. I imagine he is a sensitive soul. His limbs are long and attach themselves to his torso haphazardly, and he stoops with a sense of self-consciousness. They come as a family, a unit of togetherness, they seem wholesome and honest. I feel a bit deviant in comparison. This table has seen some wild parties and could tell some stories but it started its life as my family table, working class, white with a small drop of aspiration.

I glance around the room, wondering if there's anything that betrays my life of glamorous sin. The boy looks over at the IKEA bag of wigs, sparkly costumes, makeup and electric cables by the front door. I see him looking around in wonder; he takes a quick burst of air as he looks around the room and then back at the IKEA bag. It's unnerving, the family seems out of place here, so I ask if they'd like a cup of tea whilst showing them the table. They politely decline.

I have no milk in the fridge and I really need to do a big shop.

I point at a cigarette burn in one of the chairs and tell them, 'It doesn't extend to a six-seater table anymore, the special hinge is broken.'

They carefully look it over.

'What do you think?' I ask, casually giving them an option to tell me if it's not really for them. I mention that the backs of the chairs are loose. I wonder if I should really be giving this away.

Without saying a word to one another, Jeevanee says they definitely want it. They fetch a screwdriver from their car. They hand it to the boy, who immediately crawls under the table and begins taking it apart. He seems to know exactly what he is doing.

Together, the four of us carry everything to the car – four chairs, the tabletop and the big, heavy, carved-wood base. I feel like their second son, the impractical wayward one.

I retie the cord on my dressing gown and rush back inside to grab the screwdriver they have left behind.

They drive away and I'm alone again. I think about this family, strangers in Bristol. My table and chairs, once central to my life, will now be the focal point of theirs. I wonder if the boy might think of me when he sits down for tea. I wonder if he will grow up to be queer like me. I wonder if he'll feel embarrassed when his dad makes a naughty joke.

I wonder if his mum might make him a favourite meal and serve it to him, when he shares his true identity.

I sit at my new table and chairs – the remaining set – and hope they'll be happy. Then I just cry and cry.

Tom Marshman has been a performance artist for 25 years, producing over 60 projects across different mediums. Tom is now developing a memoir and moving into non- fiction, previous work featuring in *The Haunting of Ashton Court* (2023). An overarching theme is that of the outsider and their story, particularly LGBTQI+ experiences; stories that have been omitted through archival silence.

Told You – Catherine Lockhart

When I tell them
who I am,
I'll think briefly
of you
and I'll wonder
what you might have said
if I'd had the chance
to tell you too.

Catherine Lockhart is a queer author and poet based in the West Midlands. Her short story, *Village of Rainbows* was published in *Night Time Economy* (Floodgate Press), and her poem *Shrink* appeared in Heroica's *Body Odyssey* anthology. Her work explores themes of grief and mental health, nature, and queer community, friendship, love and history. catherine-lockhart.wixsite.com/author

Sea Change – Graham J Sharpe

July 30th 1978

It is the day after my twelfth birthday.

We sit on the swings under a blue sky divided by aeroplane vapour trails. Yesterday's freshly cut grass has turned in the humidity, the sweet scent of summer soured and fermenting. Only 10 a.m. and the back of my neck already roasted. Matt and Simon promise to keep in touch, but I know from experience that long phone calls are expensive and letter writing is homework.

Dear God, it's Gregory Green, I'm a member of the local church choir, you might remember I set my hymn book alight at the carol service on Christmas Eve. Please can you seal my tear ducts for the next twenty minutes and save me from embarrassing myself? Sorry to be a pest. Grandma Green says her prayers don't go further than her bedroom ceiling, but I have faith in you. And, if you created the Heavens and Earth in six days this isn't much to ask.

Thank you, oh Lord. Amen.

'Did you watch *Charlie's Angels* last night?' I say, filling the silence.

'Definitely,' Simon says.

'Who's your favourite?' Matt says.

'Bagsy I'm Sabrina,' I say.

'What do you mean?' they both reply.

'If we're playing a game of *Charlie's Angels,* I'll be Sabrina,' I raise a hand to stop them interrupting, 'yeah, I know what you're thinking, she's not as glamorous as Jill or Kelly, but she's the smart one.'

'Playing a game?' Simon sounds horrified.

'What planet are you on?' Matt plants both feet on the tarmac. 'Which one do you think about at night?'

'At night?' I slide my hands down the chains. Reduce my speed. Make eye contact with Matt to gauge his expression. 'I don't know what you mean.'

'You are kidding, aren't you?' Matt looks astonished.

'Um.'

'We mean,' Simon brings his swing to an abrupt halt, 'which one would you screw?'

'You know,' Matt thrusts his hips forwards, 'have sex with.'

'Oh, that,' I try to laugh, but it comes out strained and desperate. 'Obviously, I'd screw them all.'

Matt and Simon double over with laughter. My stomach lurches, and not just with shame. An innate and unspeakable yearning, coiled deep inside of me, sensed but unrecognisable until this moment, has revealed itself. I stare down at my Clarks sandals.

This stupid park, created to celebrate the Queen's Silver Jubilee, used to be a field. Now it's a field with four swings and some unpleasant surprises. After the celebrations the council stopped collecting litter and the locals unleashed their dogs. No one rolls among the dandelions a second time.

The smell of the metal on my palms reminds me of all the times we spent here. For three and a half years we did everything together, but Matt and Simon have already signed up for karate classes without me. Awkward conversation drags on for several minutes. Perhaps the absence of a shared future makes communication difficult. Maybe my stupidity has rendered our friendship impossible and they can't wait to escape. Unable to bear the strain, we say goodbye earlier than planned.

By the time I get home the removal men have rolled up the carpets. While they load them into the giant blue Pickfords lorry we drift through empty rooms for one last look. Without our things, the house has died. The walls are bare, the rooms echo. The lounge floor, where I used to sprawl after school, watching cartoons and eating biscuits, is cold, hard concrete now. The windows are still in the same place, but nothing feels right.

We're ready to leave and lots of our neighbours have gathered to wave goodbye.

Sally, from number twelve, leans into the car and squashes my face in her hands. 'Sorry about the garlic,' she says as she presses a wet kiss on my lips, 'I'm cooking Bolognese sauce for the freezer.'

Without access to antibacterial soap and a hot flannel I must wipe her saliva on my T-shirt.

'Bel, for heaven's sake,' Bernie drums his fingers on the steering wheel, 'we don't need the waterworks.' He turns to me and my brother, 'she's just prolonging the agony.'

Bel and Sally are hugging and swaying on the pavement

like drunks doing a slow dance at the end of a party. Bel untangles herself and jumps into the car.

'Get on with it then,' she says.

Sally blows her nose into her tea towel. Bernie puts his foot down and abrupt acceleration pushes the back of my head into the seat. Up to the age of ten I would get car sick, and puking out of a window at ninety miles an hour is the perfect way to test all five senses at once. We keep the windows down and wave until we turn the corner, speeding through the small Cheshire village that isn't ours anymore. Past the pub, the scout hut and the chippy that has scampi on the special menu. Over the raised drain cover where I somersaulted off my bike and the school dinner lady gave me first aid with custard. Mickey's sweet shop disappears in our slip stream. The church, where my hymn book shone brighter than the star of Bethlehem, is on the other side of the hill.

Mr and Mrs Baker from next door have given us luxury travel sweets for the journey. They are in a round, gold tin and heavily dusted with icing sugar. My head is bursting with questions about boys and girls and what proper love should feel like. Touching each sweet with the tip of my tongue, so they can be identified by colour and separated into groups, is a satisfying distraction.

'It's the end of an era,' Bel sobs into a tissue.

A proper husband would say something reassuring. Bernie lights a Benson & Hedges cigarette, exhales, jabs a cassette into the player and Neil Diamond sings 'Beautiful Noise'.

Bernie is my dad. He changes jobs so often he could be an undercover spy for MI5; people say he looks like Sean Connery, but it's mainly the Scottish accent. In real life he sells cardboard boxes for a living. A travelling salesman who calls other drivers *fucking eejits* for being too slow, drinks whiskey with a dash of water, plays golf with a handicap of two and smokes sixty B&H every twenty-four hours. Bernie is the perfect name for a man lost in smoke.

Belinda is my mum's proper name, but everyone calls her Bel. She hates raised voices when windows are open, worries what the neighbours think, and keeps her charm bracelet hidden in a casserole dish. In the black-and-white wedding photo on her dressing table there's a hint of Elizabeth Taylor: dark hair, porcelain skin and sparkling jewels. It's possible she turned her back on Hollywood, inspired by Grace Kelly who gave up her movie star career to marry Prince Rainier. Grace is now the Princess of Monaco and, until last week, Bel was a part-time secretary for an accountant in Nantwich.

Michael is my big brother, he's fourteen. We're sitting on the back seat. Ordinarily, we maintain a safer distance. Years ago we shared a bedroom and Michael drew an imaginary line down the middle. Whenever I crossed it he gave me a Chinese burn so I stabbed him in the spine with a pencil. Another time, he hid my Lego down the side of the washing machine and when I crawled in to get it I dislodged a pipe and got covered in scalding water. The only thing we have in common is hospital visits.

For the past few days Michael has been killing me with car facts: Ford Granada Ghia, Jupiter red, beige vinyl roof, tan velour interior. It probably kept his mind off the move. The thing I love most about the new car are the seat pockets because they remind me of aeroplanes and our holiday to the Costa Brava.

One day I will be responsible for in-flight comfort and safety.

Standing in the aisle with my nose in the air pointing out the emergency exits. Maintaining an air of calm professionalism when there's no more chicken. Marching up and down the cabin dispensing hot beverages saying things like, 'Pop your cup on the tray.' Bel's cousin is an air steward with British Airways; he flies long haul and he's had his hair permed.

'We're taking the scenic route,' Bernie says.

Bel's head is lolling in circles.

Despite knowing we've got hours to go, I can't resist saying, 'Are we nearly there yet?'

'Shut up,' Michael says.

'You bloody shut up.'

'Both of you shut up,' Bernie raises his voice, 'and less of the language, Gregory. I do the swearing.'

Bel's head jolts to attention. 'Who's swearing?' She unfastens a button on her blouse, pulls down the sun visor, wipes away the black smudges from under her eyes and arranges her hair in the mirror. She applies a coat of lipstick (probably Cherry Frost by Max Factor because that's her current favourite). Usually, she blots her lips on tissue paper, but today has lost all regularity.

The scenic route to North Devon takes us across Exmoor. An empty road snaking its way through a barren expanse of greens and browns. There aren't many trees, and those that have survived look stunted and wind beaten. We tear through remote hamlets and screech past lonely stone houses. Bernie says it's stunning. He's wrong. It's a bleak and lonely place and the thought of living here makes me anxious.

'You're going to love the sea,' Bernie says.

Really? You think so? My anxiety turns to anger. Will

I find a cure in salt water? Or a message in a bottle with instructions on how to behave like a normal boy? Bernie lights another B&H and blows smoke into silence.

Our new home smells like sour milk. Bel says it belongs to the previous occupants and I wonder if our family has a smell and if we left it behind. The family before us also left dust (which is ninety percent dead skin cells), matted hairs in plug holes, stains in toilets, nails in walls, scuffs on skirting boards, a carving knife behind the boiler in the kitchen, fluff where there used to be a washing machine, a slice of rock-hard toast under the grill and, hidden on top of a wardrobe, a magazine called *Mayfair* which immediately vanished.

'These objects are clues,' I say.

Bel clasps her pink marigolds together as if she were praying. 'What are you talking about?'

'The leftovers help us to create a picture of life in this house before we arrived. Maybe the knife behind the boiler is a murder weapon.'

'I feel like murdering someone,' Bel says.

Living in an old house is a new experience. A pantry in the kitchen, a fireplace in the lounge, big, clunky light switches and some of the electric sockets only have two holes. There are rusting metal window frames and earwigs drop from the hinges every time one is opened. All four bedrooms have a sink, which is another novelty. Apparently that's common by the seaside because people like to do Bed and Breakfast.

'Will we rent out our spare room to tourists?'

Bel shakes her head, 'Absolutely not.'

Bel's cleaning frenzy shows no sign of abating, so I drift

outside and loiter under the veranda at the back of the house. The patio wall has seen better days, and gouging out loose mortar is highly addictive. I have already received my final warning. Overgrown with ivy and partly submerged beneath a tsunami of nettles and brambles, it's high on Bernie's to-do list. But Bernie's DIY skills don't reach further than superglue, so a transformation is unlikely.

Bel appears on the veranda gripping a coffee. 'This house is squalid.' She pulls a tissue from her sleeve.

'Don't cry,' I say. 'It'll be alright.'

'No, it won't. Life isn't a cakewalk, that's what your great aunt Maureen always says.'

'What's a cakewalk?'

'I don't know.' Bel blows her nose. 'It's just an expression that means life is hard.'

Looking down, over fields, treetops and slate roofs, the sand dunes appear mostly green. Waves of marram grass are interrupted by occasional, sandy tracks. Beyond them, a slither of beach makes an appearance when the tide is out. The Atlantic Ocean should be the star of the show, but it often merges with the sky to create a homogenised smudge. Today's horizon has vanished in a solitary shade of grey. Despite investigating every inch of the village, on bike and foot, I still feel lost. 'Maybe you need to stop cleaning for a while.'

Bel shakes her head. 'You know that dress you were looking at earlier, the one in the trunk?'

'You mean the old fashioned black-and-white one?'

'Yes, exactly, well I was wearing that the night I met your father. September holiday weekend, 1960, The Moorings Ballroom in Largs. Me and Moira, my god, we used to have so much fun. Your dad asked me to jive.'

'Dad, jiving?'

'I know, it sounds unbelievable.' Bel's gaze drifts towards the lost horizon. 'We made a foursome, me and your father and Moira with your father's pal Douglas. Moira had it all planned. She thought she'd hit the big time with Douglas because his parents owned a hotel, but it turned out they were in terrible debt and Douglas didn't know how to polish his own shoes.'

'That can't be true,' I say. 'Even I know how to polish shoes.'

'No, what I mean is, all through his childhood he would put his shoes outside his bedroom door at night for someone else to polish. They had staff to do everything. He couldn't boil an egg and that is not the foundation for a happy marriage.' Bel turns to face me. 'Gregory, you must keep this in mind when you fall in love with a woman.'

'What if I don't want to marry a woman?' I say.

'You'll feel differently when you're older.'

'What if I already know how I feel?'

'You're too young to know about that sort of thing,' Bel shakes her head dismissively.

'So, did Dad propose to you straight away?'

'No, he joined the RAF, went to Germany to do his national service.'

'Did you miss him?'

'We kept in touch by letter. I wanted to move to London.'

'Why didn't you?'

'I don't know.' Bel's voice falls flat. 'It wouldn't have been the right thing to do. London felt like another world, I lost my nerve, your dad came home. We got married.'

'And,' I say, trying to sound cheerful, 'you both lived happily ever after.'

Bel throws her head back and laughs, 'Oh yes, absolutely.'

'But, you are happy. Aren't you?'

'In the sixties, women had to give up their jobs when they got married. The girls in the typing pool clubbed together and bought me a nest of tables. Every time I unfold one I can't help thinking about what might have been.'

'What do you mean?'

Bel glances into her cup before gulping the dregs. 'We had a distant relative who was a famous dancer. He once played the lead in *Brigadoon* in the West End. Your grandma says he was very light on his feet. I dreamt about becoming a dancer. Had it all planned, actually. Thought if I didn't make it on the stage I could train to be a make-up artist.'

'That sounds like a brilliant plan,' I say.

'It was,' she replies.

We stand in silence for a moment before Bel turns and disappears back inside.

Close to a tangle of thorny branches, something catches my eye. Suspended upside-down in a transparent chrysalis, a red insect is using its legs as levers to split the casing. I wait and watch, keeping as still as possible. Slowly, methodically, aided by the weight of a pulsing abdomen, it eases itself out. Millimetre by millimetre. When freedom finally arrives, it is an instantaneous burst of life and colour. Antennae twitch, detecting the scent of flowers for the first time. Wings unfold, stretch wide, and I remember to breathe, letting the beauty of it sink in. Metamorphosis sounds simple on paper but looks like an impossible task. How can something so fragile and intricate have the strength and tenacity to succeed? After several minutes the butterfly takes flight, dancing effortlessly across the garden. It circles back as if to say, *look at me! I did it!* before rising and heading out to sea.

Graham Sharpe self-published his first novel in 2012, becoming a quarterfinalist in the 2013 Amazon Breakthrough Novel Awards. *Sea Change* draws from the opening chapters of his nearly complete second novel. Caravan trips with his husband are the perfect antidote to thirty years spent serving coffee in the clouds.

February – Robert Hamberger

1.30 a.m. My iPhone rings. A woman asks my name and I say it. She tells me who she is, a doctor in intensive care. She says my husband Keith's operation took four hours, when it was expected to last an hour. The surgeons found a blood clot and tear in his bladder, which have been resolved. She tells me the next 24 to 48 hours are critical, asks if I have any questions.

By now I'm shaking and say, 'It's a lot to take on board.' She agrees. She tells me he's unconscious with sedatives and painkillers, on a ventilator. She says I can phone later this morning at around eleven to see how he's doing, unless they need to ring me before that.

When she ends the phone call I slip back into bed, but the shaking continues. I keep saying out loud, 'I don't know what to do.' The bedside lamp stays on because I don't want the dark. I pick up his slate-blue shirt which lies on a chair nearby. I bring it to bed with me, kiss it and repeat his name with his shirt in my arms. I know I'm supposed to sleep, but I can't stop my head from teeming with terrible possibilities. I think of telling the children. How do I say it? I think of letting his friends know. Where does he keep their numbers? I think the songs at his funeral could be the songs we chose for our civil partnership in 2009: walking in together to 'Ocean Drive', Chet Baker's 'Time After Time' for signing the register, 'La Mer' for walking out into sunlight and confetti from all our friends.

I say, 'He has to come back' several times into silence, my voice high as a wailing child. I carry his shirt when I walk to the bathroom. I need him near me. Returning to bed, I topple into sleep, rise from it, fall again.

I find myself awake before seven, decide it's a good sign that the hospital hasn't phoned.

I visit him on the intensive care unit in the afternoon. There's a tube in his mouth. He's wired to monitors, sleeping his drugged sleep. I remember this from twenty and ten years ago, his heart operations – mitral valve repair; mitral valve replacement – so I feel a little more prepared, less shocked by what I'm seeing. Am I becoming an old hand at illness?

A few days after Keith's initial operation to remove forty bladder-stones, there were complications, so this is his second surgery in a week. How much can his eighty-one-year-old body take? I sit by his bed, speak encouraging words behind my paper mask, squeeze his hand as gently as I can, so as not to crush him, maybe not to wake him. The ICU consultant says his indicators are gradually moving in the right direction. His night nurse says he's even occasionally been opening his eyes, which feels miraculous. I want him to rest, replenish, come home when he can.

That night his blue-grey shirt lies crumpled by my pillow, helping me sleep.

Our daughter Amy visits with me today, having travelled four hours from Bristol to support us. They bend the rules so we can see him briefly together in intensive care, Keith sitting up in bed smiling, wired to machines. To hear his voice again, joke with him, stroke his stubble feels unbelievable, as if he's been rescued. He says, 'The ceiling's moving.' We try to reassure him, but his nurse says he's been filled with so much medication it's no surprise he's a little disorientated. I kiss his forehead through my paper mask.

Our drive to and from hospital is fifteen miles. Afterwards Amy and I walk over Ditchling Beacon, bullied by the wind. Last week I saw and heard skylarks here, three climbing the sky, beating their wings and singing. None today, though a pheasant arrives, lord of the grass, running towards a bush and picking through leaves.

At our next visit, the intensive care nurse tells me they're giving him more blood to help his energy. I tell him, 'I like being with you.' Wired up in bed, wearing a striped nightgown, he says it back, looking into my eyes. I narrow my life to focus on him. What else are my hours for?

He's being returned this evening to Anstey ward, the crisis over. Amy takes the train back to Bristol, and the flat feels suddenly lonely. It makes me face the memory of those early morning hours, carrying his shirt from room to room. I think instead of him returning home. My priorities must revolve around him without smothering, wanting him to receive my support as something he can lean against, with no obligation, for all he's given me. I'm seventeen years younger, and can use that strength for his benefit: to help him feel safe. The possibility of loss can be held in abeyance. At 1.30 a.m. on Monday my body knew how fearful it felt, my days without him steeped in that knowledge.

I visit him on Anstey ward, out of intensive care. Each day he's looking better, in his beautiful, stubbled way. His voice breaks and he steadies himself when he says how kind people are. I say, 'There's a reason for that – it doesn't come out of nowhere.' He says, 'Maybe so,' adding that he feels 'privileged' to have me here. He feels shaky, but hopefully the physio might start tomorrow, to rebuild his confidence. The nurses think a week or so on the ward.

Suddenly he talks about how I appeared in his life with three children twenty-six years ago, and nothing could have prepared him for all the changes that my arrival made. He talks about not fully appreciating the anguish I'd been through with the end of my marriage three months before we met, how he's glad that pain is over for me. I tell him he saved my life. He says, 'If that's true, it's something to be proud of.' I tell him how hard he's worked with the kids, what a difference he made to them. He replies, 'I love them. I didn't understand about love until I met you. Of course I loved my family, but this is different. You're the only man I've ever loved.' We're both tearful, and I kiss his lips and forehead through my mask. A hint of panic swims through me that he might be saying his farewells. It scares me, but I manage to persuade myself he's reassessing his life. He says he thinks of Kemptown and our flat and St James's Street, and how incredible it'll feel to walk there again.

After the hospital I take a brief rainy tramp over Ditchling Beacon, to be out in the air again. A rook is blown above the gorse by the wind. I'm suspended, as susceptible as a bird to any weather.

Keith started physio today, needing a Zimmer frame, but proud of his cautious achievement.

I need to tell him there are seven steps down towards our basement flat, so he can rehearse them. He met a handsome young Italian doctor from intensive care, coming to check his progress. When he introduced himself at the end of the bed the doctor said, 'Hello – I'm Claudio.' Keith told me he thought, 'Yes, you certainly are.' Despite Claudio's mask, Keith said he'd stepped straight out of a Renaissance painting. There's life in the old dog yet.

Driving home, I stop off halfway to trudge over Ditchling Beacon again, to walk my confusion away. This time I come across a dewpond, virtually circular, edged by a couple of hawthorn trees, bent by the wind on either side. I wonder how the dynamics of our love might alter.

That evening, to distract myself I click into an online nature writing course, where the poet Louise Kennard says, 'It's easy for the familiar to become invisible. Walk slowly. Notice the self-seeded plants in the pavement. Each encounter can be worthy of writing about.' Can I write my way through this? It feels as if words might be the only tools I have: to build meaning in the middle of flux, to make sense. Hoping he's out of pain tonight, I prepare to reduce my horizon to two men living with age and illness. I want him to have another good night, as if each hour free from pain signifies his body carrying him towards health. I'm powerless under its process. Nothing I do affects the outcome, yet wishing helps. If our tower of cards collapses, my love continues.

Robert Hamberger has been shortlisted and highly commended for Forward prizes. He won The London Magazine Poetry Prize 2023. *Blue* Wallpaper (Waterloo Press) was shortlisted for the 2020 Polari Prize. *A Length of Road: finding myself in the footsteps of John Clare* (John Murray) was published in 2021. *Nude Against a Rock* (Waterloo Press) was published in 2024

The Half-truths We Tell Ourselves to Survive the Days – Katie Margaret Hall

What I can say:
I live in the honest shock,
the queer strain.
I remember the devoted interests
and suspicious feelings,
the curt struggle
and considerate difficulty.
I live in the outside
between every happiness.
I am not an afterthought,
after thought,
these are the hardest words.
Words that sit in the tension
of the inappropriate boundary.
I will not just settle,
the price is too high.
I proposed we take space,
you proposed infinity.

Sorry, my love; goodbye best;
wishing well; truly.

Katie Margaret Hall is completing a PhD in creative writing at Kingston University. She has been a finalist for several national writing awards and is published in a number of anthologies. She created the UK's first LBQT digital series, *She's in London*, and produced the award-winning feature film *Under the Influencer.* Her debut novel *To Autumn* will be published in 2025.

“Hey, Joan” – Natalie McGrath

it’s here
looking out over Catterline Bay
I understand part of me is on fire
nothing can put it out
Catterline Bay: a perfectly shaped curve
an ever-present crescent moon
to curl up into
        sky now blue no longer the colour of flint
                        we’ve had all the seasons in one day
                    July Northeast coast of Scotland
                    Kincardineshire
                    coats on coats off
                    rain showers making us laugh
                    whilst knowing
                    being here
                    is an epic fucking miracle
        new thoughts land
ripple between us
sway like underwater kelp forests
thoughts hewn
out of ancient rocks

fields
wildflowers
salt now lingering on our skin
our hair
our clothes
our tongues
shingle the size of a fist
making us unsure
unsteady underfoot
looked so small from above
in photographs studied
we were already a little unsure
unsteady underfoot
cancer looming large brutal on your lovely body our hearts breaking
still our imaginations captured
by paintings
bursting out of a book
a lesbian pilgrimage then
(we love a pilgrimage)
where a lesbian painter
once stood
her studio outdoors
1950s Lambretta
by her side
easel alive
painting canvasses that burnt holes in the sky
Autumn's fire
Winter's edge
Spring's renewal
Summer fields
full of rapture

longing
Scotland as a vast studio
how bold to capture such a thing
it restores something in us
this vastness
letting it all in
on the pier I say, "Hey" you release a breath that
turns into a smile
I leave a piece of me here forever
standing looking out with you
even though part of me
is still on fire

Natalie McGrath (she/her) is a queer writer who works in Devon and Scotland. As a playwright her plays have been produced and toured all over the South West region. She is currently working on her first book. This is the first time she has submitted anything to a collection.

She Came to Play – Marilyn Smith

What *am I* thinking? Walking among the dead on a day as hot as this. Madness really. In Père Lachaise cemetery the clotted air curdles the spaces between sepulchres and tombs, giving rise to the heavy odour of baked earth. Paris is burning beneath a brutal August sun. Standing in this sprawling necropolis in the east of the city, I long for the cool blue days of October when I can sit quietly on a bench at the top of the stone steps watching the fallen dead leaves turn the daylight yellow. Not for the first time I wonder if she can see me. Watching from some silent place. Like when her dark eyes would follow me from the bed in the pale naked quiet of the morning, sheets crumpled, our clothes long discarded on some distant shore. I remember the bedroom the morning after our last evening together, the air thick with the turbulence of the night. Our empty wine glasses slick with dark-red sediment and the burned-out candles balanced on piles of books. An overfilled ashtray left outside on the windowsill, a telling measure of our long-drawn-out late-night conversation. It had been intense. The issue of my possessiveness. My unreasonable suspicions. My contorted frown every time she received a notification on her phone.

Or spoke to the young tongue-pierced girl behind the bar for longer than necessary. Something about her feeling suffocated. Reshaped. Thursday had bled into Friday with raised, angry voices. A slammed bathroom door. Another Bordeaux opened, the cork rolling off the countertop to the floor only to be found weeks later and cradled like some holy relic. I had gripped her by the shoulders. Felt her tiny bones as I shook her. We had of course fallen into bed, and afterwards, I had pressed my face and lips against her smooth, naked back. Eyes closed, my fingers had traced the pale constellation of freckles upon warm skin. Leaving late for work that Friday morning, we had parted with only the briefest of kisses. Too tired, too bruised, too hungover for more. I had left the room as it was for days, unable to wash the glasses or change the sheets. Hours spent with my face pressed to her pillow breathing in the scent of her that had slowly faded.

I had met Simone in a small expat's bar in St Paul. Not my usual haunt. I was still trying friends and lovers on for size in those early days. Thinking I had met my tribe until finding the inevitable flaw in the fabric. Usually caused by some skewed political viewpoint or the gradual realisation we could only bear to be around the other when drunk. On one of those many lost Saturday nights, my thirty-first birthday to be exact, Simone walked in from the rain as if she had lost her way. The bar's steamed-up windows had obscured the heaving mass of bodies moving beneath a solitary disco ball. Drunk on cheap red wine, I was dancing on top of the bar beside a ruby-cheeked girl from Dundee, belting out the words to Wonderwall. Not unlike Orwell's deluded characters in the bistro beneath the Hôtel des Trois Moineaux, we believed we were all notable people in a world that seemed a good place to be. Yet on the mornings after nights like this, I would sit in a corner café stirring a lonely cup of coffee, searching the classifieds for language exchanges and meet-ups and wondering why the fuck I had come to this city. Simone changed all that. That night at the bar, as she stood there watching, hands deep in the pockets of her black Levi jeans, she looked right up at me and smiled. And of course, I smiled back.

I bend to wipe the dust from the marble stone with my bare hands before crouching to arrange overpriced flowers in a narrow plastic pot. In this heat they will soon turn to dried out husks and crumble to nothing. I open the little sachet of plant food the florist had pressed into my hand with a hopeful smile and pour white powder between the stems. It will make them last that little bit longer, she had said, and I'd nodded as if I believed her. I stand and look down at the slab of grave. A fresh, tasteful arrangement sits close to the headstone. I crouch down again to read it. I recognise the familiar looping curlicues on the handwritten note. *Tu me manques toujours.* Even now a stab of jealousy at its intimacy. Paris Pride, late June 2008, the day we met Vivienne. Bar hopping post-parade with friends on rue des Archives, people spilling out over the pavements, filling the streets with beer bottles in hands, or sat sipping cocktails beneath the hanging rainbow umbrellas at Les Marronniers. Narrow-hipped boys whipping by en route to the Cox Bar where the jostling bears held their ground. The night-tripping tourists stared wide eyed at the beauty queens who sashayed down Temple Street while smoking femmes leaned into smooth muscular arms. Furtive hands feeling hot skin under vest tops and tongues down throats as everything moved closer to the dancing girl in denim shorts and orange Caterpillars. She was energy and air, and she grabbed our hands to pull us into her orbit. We started talking. Exchanging numbers. Vivienne's hand pressed into Simone's back guiding her through the crowds. Vivienne's lips brushing my cheek as she leaned in to talk. The three of us feeling wild and immortal, the throbbing bass beating through us as the DJs sent Electro House music blasting high up into the Marais night.

The funeral had taken place at the end of a wet November. A grey pallor hung over Père Lachaise as friends and family huddled beneath black umbrellas. Her mother had insisted on a burial, a strange decision to make for someone who had lived an untethered life. Once, in a moment of reflection while a group of us was hiking in the Lake District, she had talked of wanting her ashes to be thrown from the top of Scafell Pike. Even I agreed it would be cool to dance on the wind for all eternity and never come down to earth. But that November the family had swooped in and taken back control of their once errant daughter and her wishes were ignored.

I hear footsteps on the cobblestoned path behind me and turn to see the arrival of a retired couple. They wear matching khaki shorts and vest tops teamed with stout walking boots. Flanked by looming grey stone crypts, the husband holds aloft a map of Père Lachaise pinpointing the burial places of the famous dead. I remember a Sunday morning visit to the market at Place des Fêtes one spring. Sitting on the stone steps overlooking the square, we soaked oysters with lemon juice and swigged sauvignon blanc from little plastic cups. Simone suggested we head to Père Lachaise for a spontaneous queer tour of the cemetery. We bought tiny bunches of purple violets from the market to take with us.

Once there, a tipsy, theatrical Simone, arms high in the air, welcomed us smiling to Père LesGays. Vivienne gave a triumphant little shout when she found the grave of Stein and Toklas, while Simone led the way to the tomb of the artist Rosa Bonheur buried alongside her lovers, Nathalie and Anna. Simone did not need a map. I smile at the memory. The woman in khaki shorts gives a little cough while walking towards me. She hesitates, to consider perhaps if asking for directions from someone alone at a grave breaches some unwritten human etiquette. Apparently not.

'*Pardon Madame, désolée de vous déranger . . . on recherche la tombe de Chopin.*'

At her enquiry I rise from my crouched position with some difficulty. Feel the sweat dripping down my back. I adopt an amenable head tilt to disguise my irritation, a gesture reminiscent of my mother. The woman glances briefly at the gravestone, taking in the significant details. I have no idea how to find Chopin's grave in this vast place and tell her so. I can picture Simone standing beside it that Sunday in spring, the white statue of Euterpe rising above, telling us the story of Chopin's heart. About how his body lies here in Paris but his heart was taken to his Polish homeland. I remember the look on Vivienne's face as she watched Simone talk. Not only the dead bury their hearts elsewhere.

On hearing my accented French, the woman asks if I'm American. Twenty-three years living in Paris with a Frenchwoman and I still can't escape the sense of not belonging.

'No, Irish,' I reply. My voice sounds flat and unused.

'Ah we adore Ireland!' she exclaims, with a nod towards the man now fanning himself with the map. 'Which part are you from?'

'County Kerry,' I reply, in the hope that will bring an end to it.

I feel my phone buzz in the pocket of my shorts. I turn away from the woman with a curt nod and she wishes me a cheery *bonne journée*. A text message. *Can we meet?* Terse. Direct. As if no time had passed between standing at this graveside together three years ago.

I walk to the gate on the eastern side to head home, not daring to look back at the ghosts who watch me go. It is with some relief I soon step back into the shade of the apartment on the Avenue Gambetta. I drop my phone and keys on top of the piano. Tall plane trees impose at the window casting bottle-green shadows across the parquet. The air is stale but cooler than the stifling street. A distinct smell of mothballs comes from the large rosewood armoire. I'm not sure why I keep it, but where else would I store my sheet music? I unbutton my pale-lemon shirt, regretting the sweat stains I know are visible. Have I time to change? Or better still to shower. I walk to the window and open it wide into the salon inhaling only warm air. Leaning heavily on the ornate wrought-iron balustrade I light a cigarette and watch the street. A star-shaped crossroads lies below. The neighbourhood is quiet, no different to the others during the August *fermeture*. My eyes drift to the large firehouse on the corner of the Gambetta and rue St Fargeau. But today is not the day for idly waiting for a glimpse of the young firefighters. I grab my phone from the top of the piano and punch a reply. *Yes. Café St Fargeau. There in 10.*

She has chosen a table at the back of the quiet, shaded terrace. The smoke curls up from her cigarette and a small glass of white wine sits at her elbow. Her dark eyes watch me as I approach. She looks older, greyer, even more beautiful than before. She stands and we kiss each other on both cheeks. Today we will not talk of betrayal. Of the lies and the secrets and the hidden moments in hotel rooms. Or about human flaws and jealousy. Instead, I order a glass of sauvignon and for a few moments we sit in the silence. I smile across at Simone and we raise our glasses to a friend called Vivienne, on what would have been her fiftieth birthday.

Marilyn Smith is originally from Liverpool but now lives in Paris. Always a book lover, she completed her MA in English Literature with the Open University. From this emerged a deep desire to write. She enjoys creating flash fiction and short stories. Marilyn has proudly contributed to the previous QLQL anthologies amongst others, and was delighted to perform her featured work at Paul Burston's Polari Literary Salon.

Picnic & Chill – K Devan

One month ago, a yes in the form of an emoji
thumbs up not even a heart
the corner of the picnic blanket is creased
as if someone has just left, that orange wine you like
leaking cold pearls of tears

Two weeks ago, a yes in the form of eighteen texts
the space just keeps growing bigger
vanishing the gifts
crushing the chips and dips
erasing

Yesterday, a yes in the form of a missed call at four a.m.
another man laughing in the background
there's a hole in my jumper
that I can't stop touching
it started small enough for only a finger

Tonight, a yes in the form of a slice of cake
saved in the fridge but slivers cut off
gradually decreasing till eventually

there was nothing left for you but a disappearing
sweetness in my mouth.

K Devan is a writer based in East London and his work explores hidden histories, class and sexuality. He is currently part of New Writing North's 'A Writing Chance' scheme and is represented by Abi Fellows of DHH.

An Unfinished Song – Ruth Middleton

Boiling the kettle only once, softly closing the cupboard doors, singing in the shower at half your usual volume, you tried to be quiet as you prepared for work that day. She hadn't slept well, only getting into bed with you as the light broke through the morning darkness. For several hours before, you had heard her humming softly, repeating the same patterns of sad chords on the guitar. You were relieved that she appeared to be sleeping when you had looked in on her from the bedroom door. In the warm bed, eyes squeezed shut, desperately trying to find a way in to sleep, she heard your whispered goodbyes. She had tried imagining sheep, counting and recounting them, as a dog, with more than a passing resemblance to her favourite childhood collie, herded them into a pen. It wasn't working. She half prayed, half bartered with a God she no longer believed in for quiet and the relief of sleep but in response the sounds she could hear only became louder. As a maths teacher she even had some complicated fractions that she tried to recite in the hope of drowning out the noise in her head. But today no prayer, sheep or algebra helped.

As you drove away, she held the two pillows from your side of the bed tightly over her ears to block out the unwelcome but not new or unknown haunting sounds.

She tried to relax.

She tried to slow down her breathing.

She tried to control her breathing.

She counted the ins and outs of each breath.

She tried to breathe.

As she feels herself nearing a calm place, what had started as the distant sound of laughter becomes louder. The laughing is closer. These voices mean her harm, 'they' have come together to laugh at her, they want to frighten her. She is frightened – the voices are strong, and she feels vulnerable and weak.

'Shush,' she mutters, 'please let me sleep.

Please stop.

Leave me alone.

All I want is silence . . .

Please.

Stop!

How can I stop this noise, the cruel words, the laughter?'

'What do you want from me?' She asks the empty room. She is rocking herself. At first, slowly and gently, now more frantically.

'It's not fair–

SHUSH!

SHUSH!

STOP! PLEASE STOP!'

The voices do not stop.

'Idiot!

Waste of space!

You're not going to win . . .'

The words get louder, coming into her head from each corner of the room. Some voices are familiar, some are not. She knows the words are true. She knows the words are false.

'STOP, please stop!'

The bedroom itself seems to be mocking her now. There are several purple cushions and throws decorating the bed. You had both liked the cushion she is holding now when you shopped together for the flat. The cushion is velvet, soft to touch. It shimmers and sparkles with small round glassy beads sewn along one edge. She hates this cushion now. She grabs its small metal zip, yanks, pulls and rips the material. She hurls the remaining cushions into the corners of the room. For a few moments it is quiet, and the only sound is her own breathing. She is very tired. Her body is very tired. She can feel every muscle aching. Every inch of her body craves sleep. She has not been sleeping well. At night the voices have disturbed her. During the days she has felt pulled apart. You have been planning for Christmas. She has heard you talking and she tries to listen. She has nodded and smiled in response to you, but she has not understood and cannot remember what you have said.

Her mother's voice now. It is quiet but hostile. 'Get up you lazy cow. Lazy cow, lazy cow, lazy cow . . . it's not right . . . you are not right . . . lazy cow . . . lazy cow . . . it's unnatural . . . Lesbian . . . no child of mine . . . unnatural . . . no child of mine . . . unnatural . . . over my dead body . . . no child of mine . . .'

Another voice: 'Its sick. You are sick. You are perverted.

You are sick.' Staccato bullets of words find their target deep inside of her. She tries to argue with this outpouring of spiteful and unkind words, but her own voice is no more than a whisper. They threaten to do horrible things to her, to her body. She fears that she will break and that her naked, thin, skeletal self will split into many pieces. She doesn't want to argue with them and what they are saying anymore.

At work you are in the kitchen, chatting to your line manager about a concert you both hope to buy tickets for. As you stir sugar into your second, maybe it is your third, coffee of the day you think of her. You imagine her at home still sleeping. She is not a morning person. You smile as you imagine her bed-head hair, frizzy, her blonde highlights growing out. You think that she has been somewhat distant lately. Perhaps a little preoccupied but she doesn't seem to be ready to speak about whatever is on her mind. You know that you should try a little harder to get her to talk and share her troubles.

At the flat she is not quite sure why, but she knows that she must get out of this room. She must leave everything behind. She spots an old woollen hat and pulls it on, down, over her ears. The voices are muffled for a moment and then they start again, their volume rising like an orchestra tuning up. She shakes her head, moves it back and forward trying to find silence, a moment of quiet. She is moving on the tips of her toes now. She jumps forward trying to make it across the room in as few steps as possible. She has knocked a vase of flowers onto the floor. The vase is broken but she hasn't noticed this. A moment later and she is crouched on the window ledge. Who would have thought that anyone could balance on such a thin ledge? Somehow, she seems to be smaller now, taking up even less space than usual.

She has pulled back the curtains and carefully lifted the sash window ('original,' the landlady had claimed) and she jumps. She has escaped into the overgrown, uncared-for back yard.

When you get home that evening the flat feels immediately cold. Not just because the heating hasn't been turned on, or because she is obviously not there but because behind the billowing voile curtain the window is fully open. You can't make sense of what you see. The broken vase, flowers strewn across the carpet, an empty bed, the cushions and pillows out of sight. Has she been hurt? The air itself seems to taste of mystery and of danger. As you walk around the flat you think how rare it is for her to leave her guitar, you see her purse and realise that she has left without money. There is her notebook with scribbles and words printed in capitals, UGLY, HATE, HURT and SORRY repeated again and again. You are her lover; you share this flat. You share your lives. You don't know what to do next. Together for eight months, you have agreed not to introduce each other to your respective families. One family is Catholic, one family is homophobic. You are frightened. To find her will be a challenge. You have friends. You ring them and, struggling to stay calm, ask if they have seen her today. No answers, no leads. You have to find her. You feel a growing desperation. It is late now. It is dark and it is very cold. Surely you think if she could, she would have come home by now.

The next day you travel to her bedside. She is sleeping now. She is asleep in a hospital bed. This is not a sleep that you can easily rouse her from. It is the sleep which comes to someone after an injection of heavy sedatives. The medication and injections will mean that her memories of this time are never very clear, always a little fuzzy and not to be completely trusted. You will learn to live with this uncertainty. You are her lover. You are not her next of kin. You are not able to visit her in hospital without her parents' permission. You will have to visit her in this cell-like room, in the ward with its locked door, only opened by the staff who walk around with bunches of heavy keys jangling from their belted waists.

The hospital has beautiful grounds; there is cattle in the fields and the building has turreted, fairytale towers. After some months you will be able to walk in the gardens together and she will tell you that they are maintained by patients as part of their rehabilitation. The hospital is many miles away from where you and she live. The hospital is near the town where her parents live in her childhood home. This is where the police brought her. She will tell you stories about that childhood home and how the girl who left there become the woman you love and live with. You are her lover, you are not her next of kin and every time you ask her parents for permission to visit your lover, you use the words 'my friend' 'please' and 'grateful'. Every time you ask the nurses for permission to go for a walk with your lover you promise to keep her safe and to report back any 'odd behaviour', anything which indicates that she is still hearing voices. The medication has made her movements jerky, and she walks more slowly. Your lover looks sad. You do not hold hands or show affection when others might see. She is afraid of others knowing that she is a patient in a 'loony bin' so you have told no one. For many months you have asked yourself what you could have done differently. As if she were a car and you were responsible for checking the oil levels and had not noticed that the filters were clogged up and would shortly stop the car from working. Her father maintains that you have caused her to break down. At first, you try to argue with her father. Then you give up and stop explaining how you would do anything you could to keep this most precious woman safe.

In the decades that follow you and she will meet up in cafes, in bars, to have a meal together, to take a weekend break. Books will be exchanged as will tales from your lives. You will swap news of the partners who have come . . . and gone. There will be some laughter and there will be tears.

A few years back you showed her the sales particulars for a new flat, part of the development where the hospital in Bristol had been. You both said that you would like to visit and have a look but not to live there. You didn't make any firm plans and time moved on.

Two weeks ago, you saw each other at a fundraiser for the local mental health centre. Elizabeth, who had fled through the window, invited you to join her and her 'other half' Sharon. They volunteered with the LGBTQ+ survivor group. Sharon was an outdoor pursuits enthusiast and loved going for rambles where the group members chat and support each other. Elizabeth was a relatively new, but very enthusiastic, convert to hill climbing and long-distance running. They tried hard to persuade you to sign up for a fundraising abseil, but you repeatedly said no. You promised a donation instead.

As a watercolour artist you were asked to judge the art competition and you were blown away by the quality of the work – paintings, tapestry, sculpture, a beautiful ceramic pot. Jim, the other judge, got you both steaming mugs of coffee when you met to share your thoughts. Elizabeth joined you with a plate of biscuits. Jim smiled at the two of you and surprisingly asked whether you had lived on Lincoln Street in the late 80s. Yes, you confirmed as he pulled out a photo of his younger self. Initially it meant nothing to either of you until you realised Jim was standing in a rough patch of overgrown bushes, posing next to the window of your old flat.

Jim began, 'I didn't really know the others in the block. We were all renting. Most of us in our early 20s I'd say, but we kept ourselves to ourselves.' You looked across at Elizabeth; she was looking composed but had pulled her hat further down her head. A sure sign that she didn't want the world to see her or that she didn't want to see the world. Jim's voice was gentle, reassuring. 'All I'd seen from your flat was you coming and going. Up early, suited for work but with a great sense of style when you got dolled up at a weekend. I don't remember much from that time. But I do remember this day: I was waiting in for a new fridge to be delivered. It was a bright day, the sky was blue, but it was cold. One of the days which leaves you in no doubt that winter is just around the corner. You would have long gone to work and when I looked out of the back window, there was Elizabeth. Not that I knew your name then. You seemed to be very distressed. I think you were holding a bedspread, one of those candlewick ones, around yourself. I know that you had a hat on, a woollen pom-pom one, probably hand knitted and you had that pulled down.' Elizabeth laughed gently 'That was definitely me, then.'

'I came down quietly,' Jim continued, 'I didn't want to startle or frighten you, just to check that you were OK. You were clearly upset, and you were shouting for someone, or something, to go away. At first, I thought it was the horrible man from upstairs. He didn't like "the gays" and he made that clear. But I think these voices were in your head.'

Taking the nods of you both as confirmation Jim explained how he tried to reassure Elizabeth, explaining that she was in no danger. He saw that Elizabeth had nothing on her feet and that she had caught her leg on a bramble or some shard of glass, a few small drops of blood were pooling around her ankle.

'I didn't really know what to do. I had to go back to the flat to phone for help. The emergency operator said that they would send an ambulance and the police. I went down and sat with you, Elizabeth. We waited for them under the big tree at the back of the flats. I think you felt protected there and I tried to distract you by telling you about the different trees and plants that had survived amongst the rubbish there. The police were a bit rough when they arrived. They turned up in their uniforms with handcuffs, batons even. I managed to get them to turn off the sirens, but they left the blue lights on. The whole street looked like something out of *Starsky & Hutch*. It upset me but thankfully the ambulance driver was a kind chap, and he promised to let your friend know where they took you.'

'They didn't. Everything had to go through Elizabeth's parents.' You stopped your explaining as you noticed Elizabeth had a quizzical look on her face.

'Did you give me some shoes?' Elizabeth smiled as he nodded. 'That was always a mystery. My mum and dad were given my property. I had nothing with me, other than an orange bedspread and a badly kitted hat. I'd never seen the shoes before, but the staff insisted that I'd been wearing them when I was admitted.'

All three of them laughed softly and Elizabeth went on

to say that her parents had been keen to trace the owner, mistakenly believing that this was evidence of a close male friend. 'They still hoped that I had a boyfriend. Sadly, I think Mum always did but Dad changed his ways and got to know Sharon well. I think he loved her very much before he died a couple of years ago.'

Jim had tears in his eyes. He explained his own involvement with the mental health group. 'My son is trans; they have had a hard time of it but I hope they have always known that I love and support them come what may. Come and meet the beautiful Andy.'

'Thanks Jim. I can't wait to meet Andy, but first your shoes.' Elizabeth searched through her phone for photos. 'I didn't know what to do with the shoes. Ridiculously I didn't want to throw them away. So eventually I made them into flowerpots. Here they are, I made one for me and one for my oldest and best friend.' You.

Ruth Middleton, proudly from Yorkshire, enjoys writing poetry, life writing and an occasional short story. She facilitates creative writing courses for the Leeds LGBTQ+ Community Consortium. Interests include tennis, campaigning, arts for health, disability rights, mental health, user involvement and co production in health and social care. She enjoys life with her partner Janet and assistance dog, Cookie.

Girls – Tillie Bradshaw

I was teenage when I found out
that girls have pockets full of butterflies,
necks slick with lavender,
voices full of overgrowth
and dandelion seeds.
girls carry storms in their fingertips,
I feel it drum against skin and bone,
rattle like rain on an attic room.
they are scary stories told
across a campfire, catching
in throats like smoke,
supernova, starlight and sunrise,
mighty and small.
I will never stop feeling like
every girl with a boyfriend,
is out of his league.

no one is more anxious
to impress a woman
than other women.
no one more afraid of girls
than me.

Tillie Bradshaw is a poetry loving lesbian who studied Creative Writing in Liverpool, and has recently moved to Manchester with other poetry loving friends. Tillie works as a TA, and loves cats, sapphic fantasy novels and Wallace and Gromit. Tillie's poetry covers topics such as sexuality, mental health, and relationships and how it links with nature and the body.

The Saviour – L.E. Yates

I take a deep breath and say what you're supposed to say. 'Have you made definite plans to kill yourself?'

'Yes, I'm going to climb to the top of the Olympic diving board at Stratford and jump the wrong way.' She unleashes a gale of laughter. 'Don't be so fucking earnest, Sabine.'

I don't think suicide is funny but it's often part of her daily conversation. It seems to reassure Kay that she has the option, like tapping on wood.

I put an espresso pod in the machine, stand with my back towards her while my drink drips out. The drumming summer rain on the roof of the kitchen extension is oppressively loud, so maybe this is making her mood worse. She seems particularly bad this morning.

'Whatever you and that little bitch at your work think, you're not getting my money.' Kay rakes a hand through her grey curls.

'I don't want your money,' I say carefully. And then I realise what happened last night to set her off. Of course. This makes sense now.

'You don't? Is that right?' She takes a puff of her cigarette and gives me a look that contains a trace of the old look she used to give me.

I turn away, pick up my work bag and let myself out of the front door.

Last night Kay and I sat at a pavement table outside Tranga, off Newington Green. We were waiting for our tapas, not speaking, but not, I would say, unhappy when Ade stopped opposite us.

'Hey, Sabine!' She pushed glossy, dark hair out of her eyes.

'Oh, hi.' I darted a glance at Kay, then raised one limp hand.

Ade's eyes met mine for a second and whatever she saw there made her friendliness retreat. 'Anyway, good to see you!' Her Portuguese accent seemed stronger than usual. She waved and carried on down the street.

Kay took her time, lit another cigarette, before she said, 'Who's that?'

Having too much money doesn't do anyone any good. Some of my colleagues think me working in the café is a performance when they realise I live with someone as rich as Kay but it's not. Mixing chocolate cake batter, grating carrots for salads, shaking vinaigrette for my special butter-bean dish: these are the things that keep me together. Plus, I can relax at work, Kay never comes here.

I turn off Green Lanes, then pass through the gate, the Castle Climbing Centre straight ahead. The summer downpour has lacquered its brick walls a darker yellow. This place was built in the 1850s as a pumping station for the two nearby reservoirs. It has three towers and arrow slits for windows. I wave at Caz on reception and climb the main stairs to the kitchen.

'And a good morning to you.' Ade flashes me a smile along with a courtly incline of her head before she goes back to emptying the dishwasher. Each time she reaches for the cupboard, her T-shirt rides up, revealing the tanned curve of her back.

Ade is twenty-two. It seems, on her at least, an age untrammelled by the complexities of life, a shining-bright-with-promise age. Youth isn't exactly the same as hope but I've often observed they look similar. She's only been here for three weeks but I've enjoyed having her in the kitchen. I've never worked with another queer woman before.

I wonder if Ade thinks I'm attractive – I've seen the way she smiles at me and watches my hands as I chop or prise the mixing bowl off the spindle. The mirror tells me daily that wrinkles feather out from my eyes, but I can dimly remember fancying older lesbians when I was twenty, the way they wore their world weariness along with battered leather jackets, smoking with eyes narrowed. I suppose this tough patina must have been what first drew me to Kay. I can't properly remember any more.

If I let myself admit it, occasionally I've stopped half-way across the kitchen to sneak a glance at the muscles in Ade's broad shoulders, flexing and tensing as she hefts cooking pots off the stove or hauls in a new sack of onions. But I try not to think about this now and we're making batches of salads in companionable silence when I see Ade's head turn.

Kay is stood in the door of the kitchen, hands on her hips, as she surveys me and Ade.

'Can I help you?' Ade says. 'The café isn't open yet.'

'Ahhh.' Kay takes Ade in slowly. 'So, you're the new saviour, are you?'

'I'm sorry. I don't—' Ade looks confused. I get it. Kay's onslaughts can be sudden.

'There's always one. Well, you're wasting your time.' Kay strolls into the kitchen, her watery blue eyes fierce. 'She doesn't need anyone to save her, do you, Sabine?'

I don't say anything.

'The caged bird might not sing but she likes the fucking cage, OK?' Kay jabs her forefinger into Ade's apron, even though she's several inches shorter.

Ade rears back but she's gathering herself – head drawn back, raised up on her toes – to strike. 'Who the fuck do you think you are?'

I look levelly at Kay. 'Ade, would you give us a minute, please?'

'What?' Ade blinks in confusion. 'Oh, OK.' But she leaves slowly, giving me a long look from the doorway. 'Call me if you need me.'

I nod thanks.

Kay watches her go. 'Call me if you need me,' she mimics in a pathetic falsetto voice. 'Who the fuck does she think she is? And what have you been doing to encourage her?'

She's at the being-careful-not-to-slur stage. I know it too well after all these years. 'Leave,' I say quietly.

'When did you get so fucking hard?' Kay says.

She's wearing the brown leather coat she bought in Milan four summers ago and looks smarter than she's done in months. It unravels an unexpected thread of tenderness inside me to think of her fishing this out of her mothball-smelling wardrobe, dressing carefully to confront me.

'You don't give a fuck about me, do you?'

'I'm at work, Kay,' I say. 'You need to leave.' I can feel my agitation rising. 'Now.'

For a moment she looks like she's going to overturn the butcher's block but then she swings round and stalks out. My heart is hammering. I pray Ade has had the sense to leave the café so they won't encounter each other again.

It's stopped raining outside and I've just come in from smoking a cigarette when I become aware of Ade behind me.

'Alright?'

'You shouldn't let her treat you like that,' she says fiercely. The gold St Christopher's medal round her neck flashes in the light. 'You're worth so much more.'

I'm so used to Kay's tantrums that I'd never thought about it like that, but I can feel her words begin to open up the dark, congested mass inside my chest.

Why have I let this happen? I have no good answer. Or, rather, it's so tangled at the roots between me and Kay, I can't explain.

'You can live with me, if you need. For as long as you want.' She's close enough that I can smell the tang of her sweat.

I try to laugh. 'But you live in a shared house with, like, a thousand other people, don't you?'

'There are eight of us. So?'

For a moment I imagine myself at the centre of a cosy kitchen, the windows steamed up, younger housemates gathered around, dishing up a delicious meal, coming to me with their relationship problems; cosy film nights with a projector and a gang of us cuddled up on the sofa. The possibility of a new life flares. I give a little gasp as if I'm already running towards it.

Then another thought strikes me. 'How many bathrooms are there in your house?'

'Who cares?' Ade sketches an impatient shoo-ing that makes me feel extremely English.

I wait.

'One,' she says in the end. 'And there's a downstairs toilet. It's broken at the moment but the landlord's promised he will get it fixed.'

I feel my chest close up. There are four bathrooms in Kay's house. The thought of having to wait to use the loo makes anxiety flutter inside me. I picture myself then, sleeping on a grubby couch, hunching over to read my book in a quiet corner, while people swirl past, play loud dance music, squabble, hog the bathroom.

'Bathrooms? Who cares about that?'

'They're increasingly important as you get older,' I say primly. 'You'll find out for yourself one day.'

She shrugs.

'That's really kind of you but I think I'm a bit too old for communal living.'

'I see that woman, I see how she behaves. What does any of this matter? Getting away and being yourself is what matters.'

And when I look back at Ade, I can see her impatient disdain, her incomprehension for how circumstances might trap you. She doesn't understand the sticky threads life winds you in as you get older. And I can see her point of view, I really can. When I was a student I hitch-hiked across Europe, to the south of France, through Italy, then down the west coast of Greece, camping all the way, washing in the sea, pitching my tent in olive groves if I couldn't find a campsite, sleeping on the bare ground if I was too tired to pitch my tent. I didn't worry about anything back then.

But how can I explain to her what my life is not? How can I tell her how Kay used to be?

When I don't say anything, Ade shakes her head like she's tossing water droplets from her hair. 'When is the last time you did something totally mad, you know, just for yourself, without thinking?'

'I don't know,' I say carefully.

'Then think.' Her voice sounds stern but when her brown eyes meet mine, they're kind.

'OK then, when was yours?'

'Mine? Last night, today, every minute.' She laughs and it breaks the tension.

'No, go on. Give me a proper example.'

'OK, last weekend. I was supposed to have a date to go to Queer Britain but she stood me up so I jumped on a train instead, the first one from King's Cross, and went to Peterborough.'

'Peterborough? That's miles away.'

She just smiles, in love with her own boldness.

Didn't you take anything to read or a jumper or water or a phone charger or spare tampons because the perimenopause has you in fear of unpredictable periods? 'Wow,' is all I say in the end. 'I wish I could be that spontaneous.'

'You can! All you have to do is stop thinking all the time.'

'Right, if only it was that easy.' My laugh is hollow.

'I watch you in the kitchen, always thinking, planning, like a big spider spinning a web, you sit in the corner, doing the orders every day, checking the fridge with a worried expression on your face as if there is never enough food.'

I'm flattered by how closely she's been watching me, stung by the comparison to a spider.

We're already standing close together, so I decide to stop thinking for a moment and just let myself lean in to the heat of her body but then I pause, trembling, our faces a few inches apart.

'Do it,' she whispers. 'Whatever you want to do, do it.'

So I take hold of her chin and kiss her.

When the kitchen door bangs we leap apart but it's only Hannah, the Climbing Centre Manager, looking flustered, her hair frizzing out of its ponytail in the humidity. 'Hi, we've got a bit of a problem.'

My heart sinks. She's about to tell me Kay's downstairs, making a scene.

'The garden volunteers are all here but there's no sign of Hawk. Sabine, I know it's a pain but could you possibly spare Ade for a couple of hours to make sure they don't totally decimate the herb beds? As soon as I track down Hawk, I'll send Ade back up.'

I nod. 'Sure.' I watch Ade follow Hannah out of the kitchen without looking back.

After that, I wipe down the surfaces, sweep the floor, but, as I go about my usual tasks, I can't stop worrying what I've done is inappropriate. I must be at least twenty years older than Ade and I'm the Kitchen Manager. Maybe Ade will tell Hannah I've abused my position of power, just like Harvey Weinstein, and she'll fire me.

When Ade comes back from the garden, she's quiet. I think of all the ways I could apologise but the words stick in my throat so I just carry on pounding biscuits for the vegan cheesecakes.

We work in silence for the rest of the afternoon.

'You OK to stay late for the canapés?' I try to keep all hope out of my voice.

'You already asked me last week.' But when Ade turns round, she's smiling. 'Yes, of course.'

Working side by side, we've finished four trays of sushi rolls and three of Mediterranean skewers. I'm spraying the last counter with antibac while Ade digs around in her bag. 'We are off the clock now?' She pulls out a half pint of vodka, takes a slug and holds it out to me.

I hesitate. Kay has rather cornered the market in drinking over the last few years and my corresponding instinct has been to decrease my consumption until I've been limiting myself to one glass of Champagne at Christmas and one on my birthday.

'Go on!' She shoves the bottle closer to me. I take it, though I want to wipe the neck with some blue-roll before I drink, but then I realise how ridiculous this is – I've already kissed her. I take a swig, feel it burn down my throat.

'There we go!' Ade crows. She takes a long pull, hands it back again.

I accept the bottle but I can't handle any more neat vodka, so I find a lime in the fridge and some tonic.

We drink and drink until Ade drains her glass, tosses the empty in the bin and kisses me. I kiss her back but I know it doesn't mean much when you're young. You can do it easily. It doesn't bring your home crashing down around your ears. But I feel my body respond. Yes, yes, I think.

'Come with me,' Ade says.

'Where to?'

'Must you always be asking where and why and knowing all the time?' She holds out her hand.

I hesitate a moment, then reach for hers.

'Let's go.' She pulls me towards the door.

'Wait,' I say. 'If we're the last ones in the building, we have to set the alarm.'

But she just laughs and tugs me out of the door. It slams behind her. I realise too late I've left my bag in the kitchen but the vodka insulates me from the constant calculation of consequences that creeps up in middle age. I didn't used to be like this.

It's nearly dark outside as the last slick of pink and orange fades from the sky. The tarmac is as dry as if it never rained this morning. It's humid though, still warm. Ade leads me right, instead of left to the main road. We cross the carpark outside West Reservoir until we reach a gap in the metal fence. Ade ducks under nimbly, despite her height, and I follow. She skirts the concrete lip where scrubby grass grows close to the water's edge, darting a look behind her, before she walks out along the wooden jetty. I follow more slowly. We definitely shouldn't be here.

She bends to undo her shoes, then shrugs off her white vest and kicks her long black shorts, then underwear off. My glimpse of her brown, naked body is fleeting before she dives cleanly into the water. I look around, nervous that the splash will have attracted attention, security guards even. But when she re-surfaces, spitting water, pushing her hair back from her grinning face, exhilaration fills me.

'Come in, Sabine! It's your turn now!'

I step slowly out of my Birkenstocks. That's when my phone starts ringing in my pocket. I glance at the screen. Kay.

'Come on!' Ade waves me in.

What Kay said this morning comes back to me, before

the flippant diving board comment, about wanting to kill herself.

Ade shouts, 'Jump!' just as I say, 'Hang on, I've got to take this.'

When there's nothing on the line but silence, my heart plummets.

'Hello?' I say again.

'Where the fuck are you?' Kay hisses, so furious she sounds sober again. I listen to her rant until I can't take any more.

'I'm on my way home now,' I say. 'I'll see you soon.'

When I hang up, I see that Ade has moved away in the water as if to give me privacy. She paddles back now, smiling, but all the excitement I'd felt has drained out of me.

'I should go.'

Ade kicks her legs. White bubbles surge up from the black water. 'I meant it, you know, you'd be welcome to stay in my room.'

'You're lovely to offer but I can't live with you. It would never work.'

Despite the darkness, I can see her hopeful expression crumple. She swallows, starts swimming further out to where my words can't hurt her. I remember the shame I used to feel at being rejected when I was her age.

I dig my toes into the wooden slats of the jetty. I'm fully dressed but I feel something spark inside me as she swims away.

'Ade?' I say softly. I can smell the water, mineral notes on the warm night air. I wait until she looks round, then I bend my knees and leap forward, towards her, into the glistening black.

L.E. Yates was born in Manchester in 1981 but now lives in east London. She's interested in the imaginative loopholes fiction creates in everyday life. She has been awarded Arts Council England funding and her writing has appeared in anthologies from *Parenthesis* to *Dead Languages*. Her short story, 'Sunblock', won the Costa Short Story Award in 2021.

All Girls' School – Ennis Welbourne

At the all girls' school, everyone's salivating
over the new gardener and his revealing tank tops.
The sexual tension is thick and violent and only breaks
when someone gets stabbed with scissors.

The popular girls comb their fingers through my hair
and ask me which middle-aged actors I have a crush on.
I say, 'I like people my own age,' and find myself
wondering if I have a sexual dysfunction.

The neighbourhood boys follow me on their bikes
shouting 'lesbian' because they know I go to an all girls'
school.
But it seems the rumours are true. I hear about secret
sleepover kisses
and under the cover touching.

I haven't progressed to physical exploration. I only look.
The older girl on the bus with bleached hair
throws her water bottle at me and yells 'stop staring.'
I don't want to, and I don't know why.

I'm trying not to have a crush on the class bully,
but it's hard when she puts me in a headlock.
When we're that close and I can see her quiver,
uncertain of herself and vulnerable.

Ennis Welbourne (they/them) is a marginalised writer facilitating online writing groups under the banner Access Narrative. They work for London Lit Lab as Assistant Editor and are a Bath Spa creative writing graduate. They have been published in *Transcribed*, an anthology of trans writing, and the survivor writers' collection, *You Are Here*.

Grey Areas – Lena Procter

The grey is pouring in, a leaking pipeline between her and the sky.

'Pathetic fallacy,' Emma tells her students, as they gaze out the window at the rain, slump heads on desks, complain that they are hungry, 'the weather reflects the mood of the characters.'

Rain drums against the roof. Voices drum against her skull. Children make pointless observations:

'The date on the board is wrong Miss.'

'Oh, wow, thanks,' Emma snaps sarcastically, then regrets her tone.

In the staffroom, she eats her sandwich with headphones in and buys a coke, full fat, from the staff vending machine. Teeth like gravestones, furred with sugar.

This afternoon, a man from a drugs awareness charity is running a workshop. Emma would laugh at the irony of this, if she didn't feel like a heavy classroom door was slamming relentlessly into her skull.

The man bounces into the room; his energetic gestures suggest youth, yet his wrinkles betray him.

'From all the partying,' he raises his eyebrows and points

at his forehead, which has split into perfect creases, like a crinkle-cut crisp.

The kids stare blankly. Ageing is a foreign concept for them; even twenty is ancient. Emma prods the ridges on her own forehead. She needs to quit smoking.

Addiction has caused the man's life to spiral out of control; he describes becoming homeless and estranged from his family then rebuilding his life, piece by piece.

The children write questions on slips of paper, which are tossed into a basket to allow for anonymity. This is the final part of the session. Not long now. Emma leans against an empty desk at the back of the classroom. The questions become increasingly outrageous.

If I accidentally smoked a joint, will I get in trouble?

The students are laughing and shouting out, but she can't muster the energy to intervene.

What if you only take drugs occasionally? Is that OK?

Emma crosses her fingers.

On Saturday it had been Georgia's birthday. Georgia was Lily's girlfriend and Lily was Emma's best friend from university. Emma really liked Georgia and they often hung out as a three, spent nights together at the pub, became their own unit within bigger groups of friends on nights out, had their own WhatsApp group. Only occasionally did Emma feel jealous at how much less time she spent with Lily since she had begun dating Georgia two years ago. The night had required careful planning, deciding which drugs to purchase. Emma had sorted it, as she always did, handing a wad of notes, praying the dealer wasn't a former student: her worst fear.

In the grimy pub toilets, under the glare of lighting that

gave them all vampire-pale skin, Emma and Lily debated the merits of bombs or keys of MD directly into drinks, whilst dabbing concealer under their eyes and applying red lipstick in a colour called 'hot slut.' Lily twisted her thick dark hair into knot and secured it with a plastic tortoise-shell clip

'Does this hairstyle age me?' She asked, 'I'm worried I look like my mum!'

'Never!' Emma reassured her.

Georgia clattered through the door, blonde hair already slipping from its neat ponytail. She planted kisses on their cheeks, her breath sugar-sweet with rum and coke.

'Happy birthday gorgeous! Are you having fun?' Asked Emma.

'With you guys? Always.' Georgia readjusted her black silk top, 'God I should have worn a bra, come in with me?' She dragged them both into a spare cubicle.

Whilst Georgia had a wee, Lily pulled the small plastic packet from her bra, 'shall we take some now?' she asked, winking.

'I'll wait until the club,' said Emma, pursing her lips, then instantly regretting it. If she wasn't careful, the drugs would run out. Her friends were never good at pacing themselves. Lily scooped her key into the packet and dumped the grey, gritty powder into her and Georgia's drinks.

Huddled under an umbrella, Emma and Georgia tripped down the street to the club, past soggy cardboard boxes and crushed fruit from the market that day. Georgia whimpered about how hard she was coming up and demanded a cigarette. Lily had stayed behind at the pub to round up the rest of their friends.

They paused in the doorway of an empty shopping mall. Georgia, whose hands were shaking, dropped the cigarette Emma had rolled her into a dirty puddle. A homeless man, curled up in the corner under a filthy blanket, grunted in his sleep.

Georgia was not OK. Her eyes gaped black holes and she was struggling to stand.

'I feel sick,' she swayed, leaning heavily on Emma.

It wasn't fair: having looked after children all week, if anyone should be fucked, it was her, but instead she put her arm around Georgia and they followed the distant throbbing of the bassline towards the grimy converted railway arch.

Emma thought about how clubs loved to allude to their industrial roots: bagel factory, carpet shop, bike warehouse. Where people were once paid pennies to sweat over machinery, bankers now dripped money onto dancefloors. At least this was a queer night, meaning the usual techno-loving men, aggressively claiming the dancefloor in their baseball caps, anoraks and Gore-Tex shoes would be elsewhere.

It was unlikely that the club would let Georgia in. Her eyes were closed and her entire head was tilted backwards. Emma attempted to fluff the strands of blonde hair that were stuck to her sweaty forehead whilst her jaw swung from side to side, letting out a faint but audible click.

Water and chips seemed like the best option. In the shop, a group of girls were drunkenly singing, skirts riding up, exposing pink lace underwear, ketchup smeared across cheeks.

'I feel good now,' said Georgia dreamily, 'you should take some.'

There was logic in this. At least Emma would be on a similar level. She bought a can of beer, scooped powder into it, then licked the key, wincing at the tang of metal and bitter chemicals.

'Wreck-head. How are you a teacher?' Georgia grinned, flopping her head onto Emma's shoulder.

'Only way to stay sane,' she replied, 'now eat your chips.'

The club smoking area, next to the entry queue, was packed with muscular men in tiny shorts and leather harnesses and women with cropped, dyed hair, oversized coats, platform boots. Clouds of fruit-scented vapour hung over them. Voices echoed across the cobbled courtyard.

Although the bouncer eyed Georgia suspiciously, she gave a curt nod. They handed their coats to a sullen girl in the cloakroom, who had a shaved head and ears threaded with stacks of silver rings, then headed towards the dancefloor, which was pulsing promise through the club walls.

Waves of bliss began to swell through Emma. Grabbing Georgia's hand, she followed the beat, which grew louder, vibrating through her. They threaded through the sweating bodies to the front, where the music drenched her in sensation. Every particle in her body felt joy.

Radiators in overdrive have steamed up the classroom windows. A fog of adolescent sweat, blended with cheap perfume, looms. Emma dreams about being at home: sagging into the sofa, curling under blankets, wallowing in mind-numbing TV.

'*What are the effects of MD?*'

The man describes a pleasurable sense of lightness and feelings of love.

'But the next day,' he continues, 'and for several days

after, you come down from this high and you feel ill and depressed.'

Emma's brain is thick. Thoughts mulch indistinguishably. Her body aches with exhaustion. Yesterday, she thought that she had escaped. But Tuesday is always the worst. It's unfair that a substance, which at the time made her feel pure elation, is now making her feel like she has been runover and is dragging around the ghost of her former self.

On the dancefloor, they found Lily, who added another scoop of powder to their drinks. They all held each other, expressing their feelings of love which flowed out of them. Time evaporated, as the music reverberated through Emma's body.

They went to the smoking area, where the graffitied walls cocooned them. Georgia cornered a sweet looking gay man with a thick moustache, wearing a T-shirt that said 'Homoerotic' in sprawling pink letters.

'You know, sometimes I feel like the only thing we should be doing is trying to fix climate change,' Georgia said, whilst he nodded agreement.

'I've decided that we are both queer icons,' Emma said to Lily.

'Definitely,' Lily replied, and they hugged whilst repeating the love that swirled around them.

Huddled together, they reminisced about the first time they had taken MD. Emma had spent over an hour on the fire escape outside the warehouse party, chain smoking and convinced she was going to die. Lily had been the one to talk Emma down and had cradled her whilst she shook with fear.

'I love you so much,' Emma repeated to Lily, and she really meant it.

They bought more drinks, stirred in more MD. The night sped past. Emma's body felt light, but her feet were glued to the dancefloor, absorbing the throb of the beat.

There was an unfamiliar man dancing uncomfortably close and Emma couldn't work out if he was one of Georgia's friends.

'Do I know you?' she asked, repeating herself several times, whilst he shook his head, unable to hear her over the music.

He was looking at her with concern and Emma didn't like it; she needed fresh air. The smoking area was packed with a claustrophobic crush of bodies. It was raining again; she couldn't stand still.

At the bar, she found a water cooler; she remembered that it was important to drink water, but she needed to keep pacing. That last dose had been too much. Where was Lily?

The dancefloor was packed. Everyone had vanished into the throbbing crowd. Emma noticed that she was grinding her teeth. This was bad, but she couldn't stop. She dug her hands into her pockets, searching for gum to avoid chewing her tongue. Faces swarmed around her like angry bats, flapping too close. When she looked up, the ceiling stretched endlessly.

At last, she spotted Lily and seized her.

'Why are we in a car park?' she shouted, but Lily couldn't hear.

As it was becoming unbearable, the scene around her stopped, slowed down, and came back into focus. She felt good again. Really good this time. Emma remembered that about MD. The more you took the better you felt.

Lily and Georgia were kissing and Emma watched them, happy they were having a nice time and that they were in love. Hopefully, one day, she would find this too. Emma danced with a group of Georgia's friends; her body felt fluid. Everyone else went outside for another cigarette but Emma refused to leave the dancefloor.

The music stopped abruptly as the lights came on, so harsh! The club was closing. Too early! As they found each other, Emma thought about how everyone looked beautiful, even though they were all clearly pinging, pupils wide. Georgia was telling everyone that Mercury was in retrograde and they needed to absorb this energy.

'We could go back to my house,' Emma suggested, 'but it's a bit of a trek.'

No one minded the twenty-minute walk, claiming they couldn't feel the rain. Emma held Lily's hand as she walked, and she knew that she was safe; loved. But something felt wrong.

She stopped in the middle of an empty council estate, 'Where's Georgia?'

Hard to work out how this had happened. Everyone was shivering, as the rain soaked into their skin. A friend of Georgia's was wailing about a lost phone as they retraced their steps.

The gay man in the homoerotic T-shirt was stood outside the club, puffing pink watermelon vapour across the cobbled courtyard but he hadn't seen Georgia. They wandered around the courtyard, but her shock of blonde hair was nowhere to be seen.

'Shall we check if she's at home?' Emma suggested.

'I've called an Uber,' said Lily, eyes huge, 'but I don't get where it is.'

She thrust her phone into Emma's hands and they tried to decipher the location. Emma spoke to the man on the phone but was struggling to communicate. The Uber driver grew impatient and cancelled, leaving them to walk.

Georgia's housemate answered the door, bleary eyed in his boxers. Apologising, they traipsed upstairs to Georgia's room, but she wasn't there.

They debated calling the police, but Emma didn't think it was possible for at least twenty-four hours.

Georgia's friends arrived, thinking it was an afterparty. Emma tried to explain. The friends looked briefly concerned then fell onto the bed and became distracted. Someone was singing 'Defying Gravity'. Someone was irritably drumming their fingers against the bedroom door frame. Someone was demanding another drink, another bump, a speaker.

Emma was damp and cold. She wrapped herself in Georgia's fluffy blue dressing gown, inhaling her familiar floral perfume.

In the kitchen, Lily mixed them both drinks: vodka with blackcurrant squash, poured in the remaining powder, then licked the dregs of the baggie. They rolled a cigarette, using the cardboard of the rizla packet as a filter. The harsh smoke stung Emma's throat as they gazed out at the garden, which was covered with a layer of soggy leaves. Upstairs, everyone had grown bored.

'Bit of a shit afterparty,' Emma heard someone complaining, 'wanna share an Uber?'.

She tried to explain that it wasn't an afterparty; why weren't they more worried about Georgia. Weren't they her friends? A boy with a shaved head in a metal-studded black-leather biker vest who Emma could swear she had never seen before shrugged at her.

'You OK hun? That was kind of hostile.' He blew her a kiss then followed the rest of the group down the stairs.

Emma wanted another cigarette, but the tobacco had disappeared. She lay down on the bed and Lily cuddled in next to her. Surely the only thing to do was to wait here for Georgia to come back. Perhaps her phone had died and she was crashing with a friend.

Lily was stroking her arm, 'You're beautiful,' she said.

'You're high,' said Emma, who could feel blissful waves pulsing through her again, the curve of Lily's body leaning on her.

'I mean it,' said Lily. She shifted onto her side, turned towards Emma and began to stroke her waist gently, tracing her fingers along her side.

'That's a bad idea,' Emma frowned.

'We could just kiss for a bit. It would feel nice,' Lily said, fingers stroking down her arm, shifting closer and sending electric jolts through her stomach.

'It would be weird,' Emma tried to sound firm, but desire pushed against her resolve. It had been a long time.

Face to face, eyes locked, the pause extended, stretched, dared one of them to break it. It was Emma's favourite feeling, the moment before something happened. The tingle of anticipation before wet lips and grasping hands. They held each other's gaze. Lily grinned at her then leaned in; her warm mouth tasted of booze and cigarettes. The room was fizzing blissfully. Emma climbed on top of her, wrapped her legs around her, and ran her fingers through her hair. She pushed Lily back into the pillows. Hands were now stroking at bare skin, tugging off layers of clothing.

It was easy to ignore the distant pulse of warning. She bit Lily's lip gently and ripped open the poppers on her crop top. A satisfying series of clicks and then her mouth was on

Lily's nipple. She bit hard at its pink tip and Lily yelped, then groaned, pulling her in tighter.

Emma ached with the need to consume all of her. Lily was sighing and biting at Emma's neck, as Emma pushed fingers into her, deeper and harder. Lily came with a shuddering, aching cry and soon she had pinned Emma to the bed. Now, Emma was writhing and shaking until waves radiated through her and she gripped her whole body around Lily, grinding her nails into her back. After what felt like hours of mouths and fingers moving insatiably, they lay cradling one another.

'I love Georgia,' said Lily, and I also love you.'

Emma's heart beat heavy against Lily's chest, 'I love you too,' she said. Through the waves of pleasure, anxiety was starting to nibble at her edges.

'Let's not tell her?' she suggested.

'We're fucked. It doesn't count.' Lily was biting the skin on her thumb, and it was red raw, bleeding.

Emma felt her body becoming heavy. Soon, Lily began to snore. Emma tried to sleep but every hour she found herself checking her phone time. Nine a.m., ten a.m., eleven a.m. No Georgia.

At midday, she woke Lily, who had star fished in the middle of the bed and did not respond to Emma's gentle shakes.

She called her name louder, causing Lily to sit up calling out, 'what's going on?' and looking frightened.

Emma blushed in the morning light, unable to make eye contact.

'Where's Georgia?' Lily was running her fingers through her hair, which had matted into thick clumps.

As Emma held her, she felt Lily's tears drenching her

neck. They couldn't stop shivering. The morning felt like a nightmare. As Emma gazed out of the window at the silent streets, still soaked with rain, she thought that it looked like an ash-covered, post-apocalyptic landscape. Lily called the police and left a description. This felt productive but pointless. London was full of petite blonde women.

Guilt merged with hangover. Emma felt sick, as though her stomach was eating itself. A cut on her tongue throbbed.

The faint sound of a key in the front door. Lily leapt from the bed and thundered down the stairs. Emma heard a shriek of 'Georgia' and quickly began putting on her shoes, searching for her coat.

Georgia was apologetic; the night was fuzzy: she had lost everyone, her phone, her mind, but some nice girls had taken her back to theirs. They had stayed up partying then she had slept on their couch. The girls had ordered her an Uber this morning; she was so sorry to have scared them.

Georgia hugged Emma tight and thanked her for taking care of her before the club.

'You were fine,' Emma reassured her, 'any time.' She hoped this sounded sincere.

'What did you two get up to?' Georgia asked, 'was your night as mad as mine?'

Emma tried to laugh but it sounded hollow. The room was too hot. She made excuses about a pile of marking and joked about trying to read student essays in this state. Hoping that she was imagining the look of puzzled curiosity on Georgia's face, she walked quickly down the high street towards the train station, keeping her head down, as she pushed past a small crowd of teenagers who were loitering outside the chicken shop.

'Do you wish you had never taken drugs?'

'When I was an addict, I betrayed friends, family, partners. I can never win back their trust,' the man shrugs sadly.

Emma hasn't heard from Lily or Georgia since Saturday. She's been trying not to think about it.

'Miss, have you ever tried drugs?' A student asks.

Aching tongue and gritty teeth. Still the rain drums against the roof and it's like the music pulsing through her on the dancefloor; fingernails on the door; her heart beating against Lily's chest.

Perhaps one day this student will understand how she feels right now. She imagines what she could tell them: 'Taking drugs occasionally won't automatically make you an addict,' she might say, or 'drugs can be fun but sometimes they'll cause you to make stupid choices. Oh, and afterwards, they can make you feel like shit.' If she said this, she would lose her job immediately. A sobering thought.

Acting as though she hasn't heard the student's question, she calls to the class, 'Time to pack away.'

Lena Proctor works in education and is studying a Creative Writing MA at Birkbeck. She has had poetry published in an anthology with Burley Fisher bookshop and has performed at the Mechanics Institute Review events. She is interested in exploring the history of queer spaces and nightlife. She lives in East London with her partner and her pet cat.

Seven of Spades – Felix Bill

At the western gate, an old man huddles into his long winter coat, waiting for some cue that only he will recognise. At the east, a little girl appears. Between them stands the skeleton of a cathedral, torn open to the sky. The girl looks in, small fingers wrapped round sun-warm metal bars as her shadow streams past the gate. Across the way, the shadow of the old man slips past his.

A chessboard of moss-soaked flagstones lies within, thick with shadows formed of cathedral innards and ringing with music. Unheard beyond the gates, the melody clings to every edge of stone and lingers, amorous, about the faceless fallen statue to the north.

The shadow of the little girl hesitates, uncertain. The shadow of the old man does not. He knows its moods and vices, this heap of ancient stones. Has learnt every crevice and curlicue of it piece by piece, just as he has learnt the music (though from where it echoes, he understands no better than the shadow of the little girl).

He knows that soon a table will form beneath what's left of the altar, that the last of the tower's gargoyles will throw down their shadows for chairs. When they do, he will set the table for tea and cards, and give what once he was given. Putting both hands into his coat pockets, he pulls the shadow of two mugs out from under their china counterparts in a nearby café and smiles to himself. He'd been a nervous little creature at the start of it all, hadn't he?

Behind the gate, the girl watches, fascinated, as her shadow sits down to tea. She sees herself smooth down the front of her dress, knows by the way her shadow's head tilts that she's asking a question. The girl cannot hear it, even then, for the words of shadows, only shadows hear, but she recognises the gesture. How could she not, when it's one of her own? Two crescents flash for a moment in the old man's shadow, the light, reflecting off his glasses. Her shadow throws her head back in response, obviously laughing.

The girl doesn't notice her mother's approach until she's swept up in a hug from behind. Twisting around in the familiar embrace, the girl looks down. On the ground below them, her mother's shadow has empty arms. 'Come on love,' her mother begins, 'it's time we were off.'

'We can't go yet!' The little girl is half afraid now, and it trembles in her voice. 'We have to wait for my shadow.' At that, her mother smiles.

'What's she doing then?'

'She's been invited to tea in the cathedral. Look!'

The girl's mother does not look for shadows. Her eyes are locked instead on the old man still standing at the western gate. As she stares, he raises a hand to wave. It should look like a greeting, but the man smiles at her like his heart is breaking, and somehow, the mother knows in her bones it's a farewell.

There's something familiar about the old man. Laugh lines she recognises in a face she does not. He looks a little like her daughter's father, with those same sharp cheekbones and wild curls, though his shine silver-grey. For a split-second ideas of a little girl's lost grandfather fill her head, but that's not it. The puzzle pieces don't fit. The lines of his jaw are too much like her own brother's, and the same round glasses her whole family wears perch comfortably on the end of his nose. Then there's how he's looking at them both. He looks at her like he's lost her.

He's looking at her daughter too, and in a world of stranger danger adverts and news articles about children snatched from buggies, she knows it should set alarm bells ringing. It doesn't though. This man can be trusted. Every fibre of her being tells her so.

'He looks sad, doesn't he Mum?' Her daughter asks. She nods, still trying to place that hauntingly familiar face, and comes to a decision.

'Wait here darling, I'll be back in a minute.' As she steps past the archway of the eastern gate, the old man smiles again, sadder still.

The girl knows, in that moment, without knowing how she knows, that her mother will not find the old man when she gets to the western gate. She has a feeling the old man knows why and considers asking him, but something stops her. Perhaps she knows he wouldn't say. Perhaps she doesn't want to shout over their shadow's tea party. Perhaps she's merely shy. Wordless then, she looks back to the play of light and dark across rain-strewn flagstones.

Between the gates, in that ephemeral den of shadow and reflection, the silhouette of the old man drains the last of his tea and takes a tattered black wallet from the depths of his coat. The little girl's shadow looks up, eager, and as she watches, he produces from the wallet three playing cards. Each face is starkly, devastatingly bright in the world of shifting darkness they occupy. A half-second later they're gone, secreted away in the pockets of her dress. The girl's shadow finishes her tea in a long gulp as the shadow of the old man stands, and for the split second between their human's heartbeats, they embrace, then turn away.

Outside the east gate, the girl's mother reappears, befuddled, just in time to see the old man (who hadn't been at the gate when she walked to that side of the cathedral) nod once to her daughter, then turn away. For a long moment, they both stare at his retreating figure, each alone with her thoughts. Then a small hand slips into a large one, and the girl smiles up at her mother. 'She came back.' It takes her mother a moment to remember the shadow's tea party, but when she does she smiles too.

'Did she have fun, your shadow?' She asks. Her daughter giggles, holds her hand out and angles it so that her shadow is giving them a thumbs up. Her mother laughs, copying the movement. 'I'm glad. Now, what do you say we have some tea of our own?'

*

It's a little over three years later when the girl finds the first of them. She's shed dresses and skirts by then, preferring T-shirts and a sturdy pair of cargo trousers. They're on a train, and in the slanting gold of an October afternoon, her shadow falls across her book with long, spidery fingers. The girl is too absorbed in the story to notice something slide between unread pages. She finds the card later, face down, and flips it over, curious. A seven of spades. She can't think how it got into one of her few first-hand books, and the mystery of it is enough to secure the card a place in her favourite pocket.

The second comes a year later. It's the end of lunch break and in the spring sun their shadow shifts. The youth, outgrowing 'girl' now, but not certain what will take its place, notices something half-buried in the mud up ahead. A playing card, face down. As soon as they realise, they know what it will be, and so it is. The seven of spades.

One's a coincidence, a stroke of luck. The second means the start of a story. It has to. The youth researches tarot, poker, cartomancy. Sevens of spades found face down (reversed, the books would call it) spell out bad luck and self-deceit and new beginnings. The youth doesn't fully understand, not yet, but they are starting to.

The third, he finds the day he realises. He's got words for it now, why his skin is growing in wrong. He finally knows who he is. His short midday shadow fades beneath scudding clouds, then flickers, darker for a moment, than it has any right to be. Beneath a hopeful no fly-tipping sign, in the shallows of a bin-bag sea, sits a playing card.

That third self-deceitful seven has a hole burnt through it. Fire, knowledge stolen from the gods. The point of no return. As the boy slides the third card into the smart leather wallet he's just bought himself, he knows he will not find another.

As the world turns, the boy becomes first a young man, then an old one. A handful of times he moves away from the city that raised him and twice he tries to emigrate, but first one thing, then another call him home. Ever expanding, ever gentrifying, his city is torn down, rebuilt to tear, and built anew around him. As much as things change though, the bones remain. The rain-slick streets endure in name only, but it is only in names that memories remain. The towers to the sun stretch ever upwards, new and newer, turning new to old, but the lights remain. That landmark of his childhood, the shadow-steeped ruin of a cathedral, remains. Standing in its crumbling shadow, he watches years melt and decades blur together until, quite suddenly, the old man finds himself in the January of his seventy-sixth year.

At the west gate of a cathedral's skeleton, torn open to the sky, he drinks in the amber sunlight of a summer morning lost to time. Before him, and a world away, the only day he remembers from his early youth with any clarity comes to life. Through two gates and six decades, mother and child stand watching him. As he raises a hand to wave, it strikes him how young his mother had been then. Barely beginning her forties, with decades of fate's thread spooling out ahead of her. He doesn't remember his mother's face so unlined, nor her hair when it was still more brown than grey, but he would recognise her blind.

She goes looking for him of course, leaving him to exchange a wry glance with his younger self. They both know she will not find him, but adults, proper adults that is, forget these things. It's only in life's twilight, or its dawn, that one can touch truth. Children call it magic, the old, memory. There is much he remembers that he would like to tell the girl, but most of it she wouldn't understand yet and the rest depends on what he cannot say. More than anything, he wants to tell her that they get a happy ending, for there were many years when it seemed unlikely. He doesn't though. He knows they didn't speak.

As his mother reappears he turns away, because he remembers that too. The old man doesn't check his wallet for the three playing cards he's kept there all his life. Doesn't need to, to know that they are gone. After all, he remembers how the story begins.

Felix Bill is a transgender author. His first play premiered in March, 2024, and he has had short stories published by Cursed Morsels Press, The Gatliff Trust, and Powders Press. He was longlisted for a 2024 Diverse Writers/Diverse Worlds writing grant from the Speculative Literature Foundation, and he is a National Parks New Perspectives storytelling grant recipient.

The Metamorph – Alexander Rowland

When he enters my body he does so in his own time. Only for a moment. Something quick. A hasty crawl inside before my body reacts, obligates a clench and spit, surrenders to pushing him out.

He leaves behind a mound of shed skin. Writhes his way through my guts and dumps a buried weight of peelings into my stomach. I stew on his remains. Grumble them. Boil his scraps into sleet and ready them for leaking out.

Hot soaking cakes atop the grease of muddied bedsheets and I bathe in the scum. Ponder the smells. Explore his rotting markings like a gleeful rat nosing the piss of its partners for the next crumb of feed.

I tongue any parts I can find. Digest them and seep them out again. Let my body tremble in his cold tricklings for another round. Feel his lingering.

He comes when he is ready. Fills the grooves of my strangled legs with a pile of severed fingers. Long droppings of his grips and slaps. A swarm of twitching hands that spread themselves across the meat of my thighs to heavy my limbs.

I take my time to decompose them. Give in to their scattered fingering. Let them creep for a while.

They fiddle and scratch under the gaps of my pores, stabbing through the holes of my legs with the splintering of cracked knuckles. My standing hairs weaken their stance and he collects them strand by strand. Gouges them from their beds. Claims the nub of skin at their roots as small trophies of his beastly work. No mercy of a quick rip. No sporadic whim of a curious pull.

My throat hums in the custody of his tugging. Moans for the pain his hands leave. My skin's lips sip from the pulping gape of his prickings. Oozing. A litter of open wounds that pulse and dilate and gasp for his return, greedy for his salted slathering of gashing slits.

I honour his choice to be a gloryful annoyance. Endure the sting. Submit to his gradual dismantling of my body, one hair at a time.

But tonight, he is absent. He did not leave behind some aching remains to groan for.

His pounding did not reach behind the wax of my ears and he left no burning thrust to beat against my ribs. The pearly slugs he poured into my throat have dissolved, against my will. Fell down my neck and burst like a pimple. Mutated into spit. No prolonging flavour. No slither of cud for me to lick from my gums.

Just two hours have passed since he left and I am already numb.

Where is my squirming? His dragging hands that melt from my skin? The grime that he jolts into my mouth after it begs to be fed? The lap of salty phlegm I crave to lodge in my throat and gunk aside my swallows?

I expected a grizzled chin to chew on. Some sharp odour from a pit to drink. Something disgusting to clot and dribble when I became too full to gargle and a boulder of meat to bleed through the lobes of my guts and shit out again. I have searched for him. Tried chewing the weight of his torso from under my nails, dug my teeth in, looked inside for his grit, gurned hands through my tongue to taste the gunge of his chiselling.

But he is not there.

No leftover flavours to embalm my mattress. No distant sniffings for me to belch and scab.

Tonight he has left behind a desolate spirit. Something sentient. Chilly.

When he fell out of me he did not show me the hooks of his spine, as he usually might. No boasting slump of broad shoulders sat crouched on the side of my bed, all pulsating bones and heaving breaths.

When he fell out of me tonight his body laid beside mine. Exercised its will to rest. Sponged in my paralysis.

Green eyes gave way to the weight of a neck and fell toward mine, greeting me peacefully with a smile.

I looked away. Scanned downwards to meet the blank stare of his nipples. The ghast expression of his bellybutton as it drooled with my slime. A less daunting face.

'You good?' he laughed. Broke the silence.

Took it away.

Killed the callous silence that he once had edged and left to swell. Disturbed it with a sound too sentient for the bass of his grunting or the thumps of his stamping inside. Scared it away.

He stood up and I watched his feet stumble clumsily through the holes of his jeans. I saw his wet cock cower, wriggle away and hide behind his belt. He huffed awkwardly through the dirty rags of my bed in search of a shirt. His elbows bounced through the sleeves. A scruff of hair crowned the collar, stretching through it with a sigh.

Dressed in his clothes he resembled a man. Not the monster I have grown fond of letting in.

He had transformed. Climbed into my body and found a soul to take, some skin to wrap it in. Fucked away the last of his monstrous limbs and emerged from me a man.

Just a man. Nothing less.

The type that grows weary of creatures like me. Develops a disdain for inflicting the cruelty we crave. The type that leaves me with their worst parts. Takes their best parts elsewhere. A man that walks out the door and never comes back. Discards me as a regret.

And now the memory of his leaving haunts me.

A wandering rattle. The jangling of keys from his pocket. The pattering of feet. The latch of a closing door. That beautiful man.

I am alone with his ghosts. His whimpering possession. Trapped in the banality of wondering, numbed by a curiosity for hidden tongues and eyes and overcome by a roaring hunger for his untold touching.

Loneliness. A sadism that only humans can inflict. A new kind of pain to fill the void.

Alexander Rowland's poems and short stories reflect his lived experiences of unknown, esoteric and queered realities. He writes from a neurodivergent perspective, using storytelling as a tool to explore empathy and find deeper understandings of human complexity. In the past he has been commissioned and credited in creative works for the ICA, Channel 4 Random Acts and BBC Arts.

The Locked Laboratory of Pleasure: Navigating Queer Desire in Middle-Age – Paul Taylor Pitt

What's your guilty pleasure? It's one of those questions you often see in celebrity interviews. Oprah loves taking a bath. Gwyneth Paltrow smokes one cigarette every Sunday night. Victoria Beckham watches episodes of BBC crime drama *The Capture* while on the treadmill. None of those strike me as particularly guilt worthy. I asked the question on Instagram recently and responses were similarly innocent: 'Watching *The Sound of Music*', or 'playing Magic: The Gathering'. One response does deserve a special mention. It just said: 'dark chocolate Brazil nuts and anonymous cock'.

I wondered what my guilty pleasure was. I didn't have to think for too long. I know my desires. I buy overpriced shit I don't need. Recently I bought one of the most extravagant things I've ever purchased. It arrived, a box within a box, wrapped in tissue paper, with a sticker holding it closed. Inside, a heavy cotton bag kept it safe. Each layer of wrapping felt like a game of pass the parcel where I was the only player and the music never stopped.

After edging myself through the delicious packaging, I got to the treasure. Two grams of lip balm. But not just any lip balm. This is Victoria Beckham's *Posh Balm*. At £15 per gram, it costs approximately thirty times what I usually spend on my usual brand. I could buy eighteen of those for the same price as one Posh Balm. But where's the pleasure in that?

As I held the Posh Balm aloft like Mufasa introducing Simba to everything the light touches, my husband Dan rolled his eyes and complained about the 'waste of packaging' and how I was 'too easily influenced', and 'burning money' but he has his own guilty pleasures. He recently brought home a heated mop that also vacuums.

Welcome to Middle-Age Queerness. Where the guilty pleasures are not that guilty. After almost twenty-five years together, Dan and I know each other's kinks and fetishes. Dan says he will leave me if I buy one more water bottle – I still haven't found the perfect one – and occasionally I catch him watching videos of washing machines before he slams his laptop closed as if I'd walked in on him watching Army Fuck Buddies (again). We know who we are.

We are day people, we like a brunch and a gallery and to be home by evening to watch a BBC crime drama, or sometimes we spend an hour looking for a film before watching a BBC crime drama. No treadmill involved. Occasionally we go clubbing, although those now tend to be religious experiences: Easter and Christmas mainly. We need a long weekend to recover from a late night. I realised recently I've been in more airports than nightclubs this year. This is what it means to be queer at fifty and I fucking love it.

Middle-Aged Queer Pleasure is holding Dan's hand while we watch TV. Middle-Aged Queer Pleasure is giving each other that look at 1 a.m. after we have waited three months to go clubbing, and nodding when one of us says 'shall we go home?'. Middle-Aged Queer Pleasure is a spoony nap on a Sunday afternoon.

It took half a lifetime to get here. I've always had an unusual relationship to pleasure. At school, just before sixth year, we had what was called Activities Week. Normal lessons were suspended so that us older kids could choose from a menu of fun and informative events. The jewel in the crown was 'Mediterranean Water Sports', five days in the south of France, scuba diving, surfing and snorkelling.

There was no chance in hell I would be doing that. For a start, my parents couldn't afford the cost of a pair of trunks, much less the coach fare or accommodation. That was my excuse anyway, a convenient truth. In reality, the idea of spending a week in my speedos, with a bunch of other boys in speedos, sharing a dormitory (in speedos, probably) filled me with terror.

I hated my body, my dirty double agent of a body that would give away my secret at the first drop of a towel in the shared showers. I imagined the lights going out at night to the rhythmic sound of fists moving under the covers. Someone suggests playing *spunky biscuit*, and I lose (or win, depending on your point of view). In this scenario, our hot, hairy PE teacher was also in the dormitory but he had to sleep naked because he forgot to pack his pyjamas. Oh, there was no way in hell I was going. I felt not just guilty about these thoughts, but ashamed. Unsafe. My pleasure meant danger.

Instead, I and a handful of other loser virgins stayed at school with the not-hot-not-hairy loser teachers where we spent a week on such pleasurable activities as learning

Russian, making origami swans and printing our own newsletter. It turned out to be a pretty slow news week, mostly featuring newly learned Russian words and instructions on how to turn the paper newsletter into a swan.

Meanwhile, I imagined my classmates whipping each other's bums with towels and snogging in the dark. As far as I knew, I was the only gay person in the history of the whole school so I have no idea why they would all turn into horny gay sailors in the south of France, but my brain taunted me for being such a coward. For hiding. For feeling ashamed of who I was and that all I had to show for it was the ability to say 'that is a chair' in Russian. *Eta Stool.*

Pleasure was not available to me in my formative years. While my straight peers were kissing, fingering, sucking and fucking, I watched *Brookside* and fantasised about running away with Damon Grant. Everyone else had access to this laboratory of pleasure to experiment in, sending Valentine cards and getting off with each other on the bus. They made their mistakes, casually moving from one person to the next, little people doing grown up things. Once I leaned out of my bedroom window to see my neighbour, smoking out of his. He and his girlfriend had just been fucking. We were all in the same class at school. It took me another six years to even kiss another man, much less fuck.

I didn't meet another gay person until I was seventeen. There are not many things in this world that I am certain about, if any, but I think I can say with total conviction that there is not a single straight person on this planet who can say they didn't meet another straight person until they were seventeen. They are so spoiled and take it for granted in ways I never could. Their pleasures are not guilty. They are encouraged.

Never once when I was growing up did I believe I would one day be married. It was still illegal for gay men to have sex under the age of twenty-one, much less be planning a wedding. It felt like I had my nose pressed against the windows of the laboratory of pleasure, blurred bodies writhing behind the steamed-up glass. Pleasure was not meant for me. If I did have sex, I would probably die of AIDS, which was apparently both my own fault and God's punishment because for some reason God made me gay and then regretted it? Sounds like a closet case to me. Maybe he should go on a Mediterranean Water Sports Holiday.

Mid-life is full of twists and turns. People we love get sick and die. Relationships end. Kids leave home. Jobs we once loved lose their meaning. Bodies creak and ache. Some of those are inevitable. What we do have control over though, is our relationship to pleasure. Whether it's a vacuum mop, or chocolate Brazil nuts and anonymous cock, mid-life is our opportunity to shed the guilt we feel about pleasure. Haven't we been made to feel guilty enough, just for existing?

I've been trying to feel more pleasure and less guilt about the things that make me happy. Seeing a nice bum in the gym changing room? Thank you very much. Paying for a beard trim when I could do it myself? I deserve it. Applying luxurious and lightweight lip balm that costs the same as high grade caviar, zig-a-zig-ahhhh. Navigating mid-life as queer people is complex. But we are still here, we are still queer and at last pleasure is ours for the taking.

Dr. Paul Taylor-Pitt (he/him) is a middle-aged queer making sense of the second half of life. He is a Writer, Organisation Development Specialist, Coach, Mentor, Facilitator and Podcaster. His first book *Still Here! Still Queer! Now What?* A manual for LGBTQ Wellness and Wholeness is published October 2025 by Trigger Publishing. He lives in London with his husband.